An Archite guide to running a practi
Running a

An Architect's Guide to Running a Practice

David Littlefield

AMSTERDAM • BOSTON • HEIDELBERG • LONDON • NEW YORK • OXFORD
PARIS • SAN DIEGO • SAN FRANCISCO • SINGAPORE • SYDNEY • TOKYO
Architectural Press is an imprint of Elsevier

Architectural
Press

Architectural Press
An imprint of Elsevier
Linacre House, Jordan Hill, Oxford OX2 8DP
30 Corporate Drive, Burlington, MA 01803

First published 2005

British Library Cataloguing in Publication Data
A catalogue record for this book is available from the British Library

Library of Congress Cataloguing in Publication Data
A catalogue record for this book is available from the Library of Congress

ISBN 0 7506 6099 6

For information on all Architectural Press publications
visit our website at www.architecturalpress.com

Typeset by Newgen Imaging Systems (P) Ltd, Chennai, India
Printed and bound in Great Britain by Biddles Ltd, King's Lynn, Norfolk

Contents

Foreword

by John McAslan

From as early as I can remember, I wanted to be an architect. But Edinburgh University almost killed off my hopes, with a programme of extraordinary dullness. I found myself being taught by a self-important man whose only architectural gift to the world was (as I recall) a bungalow in Duddingston which, bizarrely, had mechanical shutters on every door and window to make his wife feel secure when he was away. I never knew if this was to keep vandals out or her in.

My passsion for architecture began to flourish when I left Scotland for America in 1978, going to work with Cambridge Seven Studios in Boston. I had left Britain certain I'd never return, although 2 years later I was back to work for Richard Rogers in London, which has been my home ever since.

My first piece of advice, if you intend to set up an architectural practice, is to see the world first (especially if you were brought up in Scotland), train in the practices that appeal to you and do the work you want to do. Do not become stuck in an awful practice drawing door details.

Furthermore, I'd say don't rush into setting up on your own. Complete your training, get qualified, find your feet in a good office and, if you want to have 'complete' experiences, see a project through from beginning to end before you try one for yourself. As part of this, try to undertake everything – like winning the job, agreeing fees, getting involved in the selection of consultants, developing the design and managing the client as well as the job. And when you go off on your own and you've completed your first project, get some good pictures and do your best to get the damn thing published.

After meeting at Richard Rogers', Jamie Troughton and I set up on our own in the early 1980s. We were still young (I was 28, Jamie 31). When we sat down to consider our first project – the £180 000 Design House in Camden – we realized that our fee of £12 500 would provide an income for around 3 months. Jamie and I reckoned we needed a new job within a month or so (which we got) and subsequently a new job every couple of months. This is a rule I've stuck with ever since – try to bring in a project, irrespective of scale, every month to keep a flow of interesting, new work (and fees).

From the earliest moments of starting up, Jamie and I were conscious of the need to have simple systems in place. I recall sitting at my desk on Day One thinking 'now what do I do?' So I drew up a sheet to record the use we made of our photocopier; I prepared a template for our timesheets which, with a single job on the books, was fairly easy; then a day file, for incoming postage, and finally two further files – one for invoices, the other to record payments. All very basic. But, funnily enough, I've kept to very simple systems ever since.

For more than 10 years or so I never worried about income. With Jamie as my partner, I didn't have to learn the financial and management skills required to run the practice. But in 1996, when the practice dissolved, I was thrown into the position of having to understand the mechanics of managing a business. By then, of course, all the right systems were in place, but I really didn't have much of a clue about practice management.

From that moment I began to take a much closer (and probably too hands-on) proprietorial interest in the financial management of the practice. We now have fairly sophisticated management and accounting software and systems: all project architects are responsible not only for design management, but for the financial management of their jobs. We aim for a 25 per cent level of profitability, and 25 per cent annual growth, which we have generally achieved over the last 5 years or so.

We now have around 75 people in offices in London and Manchester. Our turnover for 2003 was around £5 million and we achieved a profit of just over £1 million – 20 per cent of which was distributed to staff, and 5 per cent to charitable causes.

When you run a practice, it's hard to remove yourself from its financial management, but beyond this you need: good accounting advice; investment in proper systems and people; to charge the right fee; to resource properly; and try to achieve growth. I have never borrowed money for the practice and I have never carried debt. I have avoided buying an office, and I've kept a close watch on cash flow.

Since setting up in practice there has been plenty of time for regrets. Here are just a few of them:

- We should have employed a practice manager earlier (we waited until 2004 when staff levels had reached 75).
- We should have invested in a good studio environment sooner.
- And while we have always received good press coverage, we have only recently engaged a marketing consultant to help shape our strategy and coach our three-person, in-house team.

The hardest thing in practice is finding enough time to think about design. After spending many years trying different systems, we've settled on a process of day-long design reviews every Monday (except every fourth Monday, which is for a management review). This gives me and other directors the chance to discuss projects at length with each design team, and agree actions. We are also in the process of defining a new post – Director of Projects – to try and ensure that all projects are better co-ordinated to precise practice standards, and that design work and fees are being effectively managed across the practice.

There is no single secret of success, but following this 10-point plan would be a good start:

- Get the right experience before you set up.
- Build relationships – you never know who you might need in the future.
- Start your practice with the right people (but don't think your first practice will necessarily be your last).
- Balance creativity with commerce.
- Be distinctive.
- Be aware that the effective delivery of your projects is key to success.
- Don't be embarrassed about marketing yourself.
- Be cautious with growth – don't 'load up' with support before you have the flow of work to pay for it.
- Put proper systems in place, and
- Set aside as much time as possible to design.

Preface

If you have built castles in the air, your work need not be lost; that is where they should be. Now put foundations under them.

Henry David Thoreau

In the late 1990s, a sole practitioner designed an expensive mansion block interior for a wealthy client. Unfortunately, for the client, the apartment suffered severe fire damage a couple of years later. Fortunately, for the architect, the client got straight on the phone and asked him to build an exact replica of what had just disappeared. Nice work if you can get it – the architect was on site while it was still hot.

Running an architecture practice is not always so easy. True, running any enterprise is tough, but the construction industry makes for a particularly difficult business environment – it is spectacularly competitive, often fuelled by cheap labour and long hours, and appears to swing from one economic trough to another. Just about every financial indicator shows that, in the year preceding publication of this book, it was only government investment in large public projects, like schools and hospitals, that prevented the construction industry from crashing into recession.

But many architects go ahead and set up on their own anyway. Earning power might have something to do with it – figures from the Royal Institute of British Architects (RIBA) show that sole practitioners and practice principals can earn considerably more than salaried staff. But this is not always the case – the same figures reveal that it is not uncommon for a sole practitioner to earn around £22 000 a year, and there are plenty who languish on the wrong side of £30k.

Running an architecture practice is generally about ambition, determination and ego. Like any other walk of life, architecture is not a meritocracy and success does not automatically flow towards the best designers. Good management and interpersonal skills play an important role. Persuasiveness is also key. The success of any embryonic practice also depends on the pedigree of its founding director. When, in 2003, Ken Shuttleworth left Foster's after almost a lifetime at the practice, potential clients began queuing up. When the much younger Ken Hutt and Nadi Jahangiri left the same practice in 1997, after working on some of Foster's most prestigious commissions, they got almost nothing (the pair, as M3, are now doing rather well, see page 28).

There is no single business model for success. Neither is success measured in staff numbers. In fact, there is a very persuasive argument that only the very large and very small practices can be guaranteed a healthy future. Some practices even choose to stay small, and will actually turn work away to avoid growth. In many ways, though, size is irrelevant: some small practices club together, allowing them to 'punch above their weight' and pitch for jobs which would ordinarily be far beyond them. Sole practitioners who have never met harvest the benefits of powerful information technology and form convincing collaborations. Others, in an effort to suggest a practice of some size, simply indulge in semantic playfulness – at least one architect follows their name with 'and associates', when there are none.

Success depends on a complex matrix of variables including marketing, cash flow, vision, the ability to open up separate income streams, the advice of a good accountant and pure luck. This book attempts to reveal how different types of practice have managed to survive and thrive. It does not (should not) offer a blueprint for success. Instead, it provides a series of building blocks, a collection of strategies and tactics based on the experience of contemporary architectural businesses. Some of these tools are the result of clear thinking. Others have emerged through trial and error. The important thing is that they work.

David Littlefield

Acknowledgements

This book doesn't have all the answers. Like Future System's excellent little book *For Inspiration Only*, this guide is intended to make people think afresh about the way they go about their business. There are too many types of practice, too many personalities, too many different ambitions to be covered by a single business model. Equally, many practices have developed highly effective ways of practising architecture, and this book is an attempt to explain and share them with the rest of the profession. Architecture is too important to be left to failing and struggling businesses; good design and good business practice must go hand in hand for either of them to thrive.

My thanks go to Rob Booth, editor of *Building Design*, who gave me permission to use articles I originally wrote for *BD* as the source material for some pieces in this book. Thanks, too, to Antonia Ward of *FX*. Also, I must thank accountant Andrew Rand, marketing consultants Laura Iloniemi and Helen Elias, architects Peter Oborn and Aaron Evans, IT consultants Justin Lomas and Hugh Davies, and Kerri and Eve.

CHAPTER ONE

Money

Any serious business, architectural or not, needs to do three things: charge the right fee, manage cash flow and get a good accountant. Too many architects make too bad a living, a problem that is largely the result of believing that quality design will inevitably lead to decent clients and a fair income. The truth is that the business dimension of an architectural practice is no less important than producing the drawings; most businesses press ahead on the strength of the optimism, enthusiasm and dynamism of their founders, but these are qualities that can take a serious knock when money is short.

Finding a good accountant is worth the effort because, as well as saving a business money, financial advice will be accompanied with a range of other services. If you use an accountant as a glorified book-keeper, you are probably wasting your money. Accountants should also double-up as business consultants and professional mentors. They can provide invaluable advice about how and when to take on staff, whether or not to buy an office, what fees to charge and even (legally speaking) how best to configure the business. But accountants, like architects, have nothing to sell but their time, so they will charge what the market will bear – that is, as much as they can get away with. The only way to make this investment worthwhile is to listen to what they say and act on it; otherwise you become guilty of what accountants call 'FTI': Failure To Implement.

'The thing most people suffer from, in business, is not knowing how to make a profit,' says Andrew Rand, a director of accountancy firm Stanes Rand which manages the affairs of three architectural practices. 'A good accountant will fundamentally save you money by reducing your taxes and, more importantly, improving your cash flow. That is, if you're prepared to listen and take their advice on board.'

In recent years, for example, accountants have been advising practices to incorporate as limited companies. This move can easily reduce a business's tax burden by 10 per cent, even for sole practitioners. And apart from that, incorporation protects the personal assets of a business's directors. Accountants can also exploit the law in perfectly legitimate ways. Once you have an accountant, ask about how your business can mix and match different legal models to help plan your tax affairs in the most efficient way possible. For example, there is nothing wrong with a limited liability partnership employing one partner as a separate limited company. Indeed, the directors of a limited company could also register separate activities under basic self-employment rules. Each form of enterprise carries different tax advantages, so you might as well try and benefit from all of them. Accountant Andrew Rhodes, of accountancy firm Sobell Rhodes, has calculated that an architect earning £50 000 a year would pay £14 655 in tax and National Insurance without the benefit of tax advice. The result of advice would reduce the tax burden to £7 925, saving £6 730. There is no legal assumption that you should pay the maximum amount of tax possible – accountants assume quite the opposite.

The same lateral thinking applies to employing staff. Practices should probably delay formally employing staff for as long as possible. Instead, it will reduce your tax burden to engage people as consultants. This avoids the need to pay employers' National Insurance. The only serious consideration is that you must ensure that the relationship of the consultant with the practice is that of self-employment. 'You do have to watch out for the unscrupulous consultant. They might avoid paying tax and, when caught, point the finger at you by arguing that they thought they were an employee and you were deducting tax at source. You haven't got a leg to stand on,' says Andrew Rand.

Before engaging the services of an accountant, you need an income, and for this, you need a fee structure. Fees are generated in one of two ways, either as a percentage of contract value (a figure which diminishes as the value grows) or as an hourly rate. It is not unusual for a lawyer or an accountant to charge £150–250 an hour, but this is beyond the dreams of many architects, whose charge-out rates often come in at around £80 an hour. Generally, practices will charge different amounts according to the level (and perceived value) of staff, and there will be a sliding scale covering partners/directors, senior associates, associates, job architects and students. Fees may also vary to match the job. Winchester-based classicist Robert Adam, for example, toughs it out and charges £150–180 an hour for most architectural consultations, but a staggering £250 an hour for legal work (advising, say, on a planning enquiry). He also pays staff overtime – time and a half in 30-min slots beyond contracted working hours of 9–5. This is, however, highly unusual. Indeed, Adam says it is 'an absolute disgrace' that this practice is so rare.

Sole practitioner Simon Foxell tends to charge a fee based on contract value, ranging from around 6–8 per cent for new-build commercial jobs with seven figure budgets to 15 per cent for small domestic work. Importantly, he tends to ignore the RIBA's recommended fee scale – which essentially shows potential clients what architects have been charging, as an average, for a range of different jobs. 'You can't really start negotiating from an average,' says Foxell, who weighs up clients on a case by case basis. 'I've seen enough clients and done enough jobs to know who will pay 10 per cent and who will pay 15. And that's what it's all about.'

When negotiating fees, never feel sorry for the client, even if you like them. If a client likes the quality of your design, or even just your general approach, the chances are they will pay for it. And the fact is that fees are only a very small part of the overall cost, which is worth pointing out if fees become the subject of negotiation. Generally, though, domestic clients rarely negotiate; it is commercial clients who always try to talk you down, but that is more through force of habit (trying to get a deal) than anything else. Unless it is your first job and you need something for your portfolio, there is little point in reducing your fees to a level at which the job becomes unprofitable. 'There are plenty of sole practitioners out there who earn a pittance because they don't see the value of what it is they are selling. You have simply got to relate fees to the value of what you are contributing to a project,' says Foxell, an RIBA presidential candidate in 2004.

Foxell recommends working for lawyers, who are generally good clients, not only because they have money to spend but because they understand, almost without question, the nature of paying fees. Also, lawyers trust an architect's professionalism and let them get on with the job; this is often the reverse of wealthy City dealers who, according to Foxell, try to retain control and do a lot of shouting. It is worth remembering that, when pitching for work, an interview is a two-way selection process and architects should also be weighing up the pros and cons of the potential client. Even a relatively smooth project will have its tricky moments, so if a new client looks like being difficult from the outset, don't take the work. This is particularly true of larger jobs. 'With a big project, you have to decide if you will come out of it feeling better or worse,' says Foxell.

Generally, this approach works for Foxell who enjoys a good living for 80 per cent of the time (2 years out of 10 are 'hopeless', he admits). Most of his clients provide repeat work and he benefits from plenty of word-of-mouth commissions. In fact, Foxell was the architect mentioned at the beginning of this book who returned to rebuild an apartment interior after a £150 television set malfunctioned and reduced his £150 000 fit-out to charcoal. Revisiting the scene not only allowed him to make a few changes to the original scheme, but the intervening years allowed Foxell to push the price up to £200k.

Figure 1.1 Boston Place, London, by Simon Foxell. A modern insertion in brick and expressed steel.

In terms of value, Foxell will generally turn away work with a contract value of less than £100 000, although he will make exceptions for particularly interesting offers or for jobs which could lead elsewhere. He applies no notional maximum, although his work rarely goes beyond the £1.5 million mark.

Figure 1.2   Simon Foxell's projects rarely go beyond £1.5 million in value, for which he will charge a fee of 6-8 per cent.

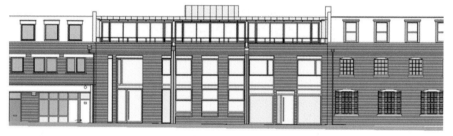

Figure 1.3 Big budget jobs attract larger and more capable contractors.

For anything much bigger, Foxell would probably collaborate with another practice, as there is little to gain from turning down work because it's worth too much. Although a £1 million job may sound daunting, there are very real advantages: design work will benefit from economies of scale (although a large building may look like a lot of design work, it is often the repeated use of single design elements). Also, larger budgets are more attractive propositions for bigger and more capable contractors.

Landing larger jobs is generally the result of reputation-building, but architects should also remember that, as the years roll by and projects get bigger, fees should also be plotted on an upward curve. It is not untypical for a practice to suffer from 'over-trading', a problem that results from a combination of increased overheads and declining profitablity. The following scenario is entirely plausible: a practice wins increasing amounts of work, moves to more expensive accommodation and recruits more staff who work longer hours; but fees remain unchanged and profit per hour begins to decline. If this process continues unchecked, the practice will go out of business.

Every year a practice should consider raising its fee, not just to keep pace with inflation but to ensure that the billing model matches the size and ambitions of the business. In fact, it is a useful exercise to ask the question, 'What would be the profit effect of an X per cent fee increase, if applied to our top 10 clients?' Then test the water on a sample client. The trick is to push the boundaries of what the market will bear without overstepping the mark. Keeping fee levels static is not an option.

Cash flow is just as important. In fact, all businesses should trade on the basis of a reliable cash-flow forecast, which means knowing how much debt you will be recovering on a monthly basis and making almost constant efforts to ensure that the money arrives. Figures for bill repayment are generally appalling: a study by the University of Leeds in 2004 shows that the average time it takes a PLC to pay its bills is 46 days, a figure which hasn't improved in 4 years. Just one third pays within 30 days; and the Federation of Small Businesses estimates that one in four businesses that fail do so because of cash flow problems incurred by late payments. Bill regularly, and employ sound administration systems in an effort to reduce 'debtor days', i.e. the number of days it takes someone to pay (see Appendix A). Finally, don't place too much faith in the fact that your invoices include a statement to the effect that interest will be charged on debts which remain unpaid beyond 30 days of the date on the bill. This frightens few people and is very rarely employed, although it is useful if a case gets brought to court. Accountant Andrew Rhodes stresses, however, that architects ought probably not chase unpaid bills themselves – this is best done by an office administrator or a part-time employee who knows that debt collection is in their job description. 'If you're the fee-earner, you should be the last person to collect debt. Get someone else to do it, someone who isn't emotionally involved,' he says.

Thinking sensibly about money need not be the miserable occupation that many in the architectural profession suppose it to be. It can even help architects answer more fundamental questions like 'What do I want to do?' and 'How big do I want to get?' Some perfectly good architects have their ambitions thwarted by spending a lifetime tackling small domestic jobs which, although barely profitable, they are too frightened to turn down. Devon-based Stan Bolt, on the other hand, does precisely the opposite and makes a healthy living by staying small and turning away anything that is not a handsome house for a wealthy client (see page 50).

Similarly, other architects are exploring separate business ventures in an effort to supplement (or even dwarf) their mainstream architectural income. Some turn to development, an exercise which RIBA president George Ferguson prefers to call 'cultural entrepreneurship'. When successful, development is incredibly lucrative. In 2002, architect Guy Greenfield chalked up £0.5 million profit from 25 flats he built in Falmouth, a project funded by his own development company Leafgate Ltd. Most of this profit was directed straight into a more ambitious, 28-unit scheme in Westward Ho!, which turned a profit of £2 million (see Figures 1.4 and 1.5). Roughly half of this will go into another development, probably in the West Country, where he looks for cheap, neglected sites in areas that have at least one redeeming feature (like a beach). His venture, which he has built up over a decade, also provides a useful subsidy for his five-person practice, allowing it to be choosy about the work it takes. 'I don't

Figure 1.4 Guy Greenfield's residential scheme in Westward Ho!, for which he acted as his own client.

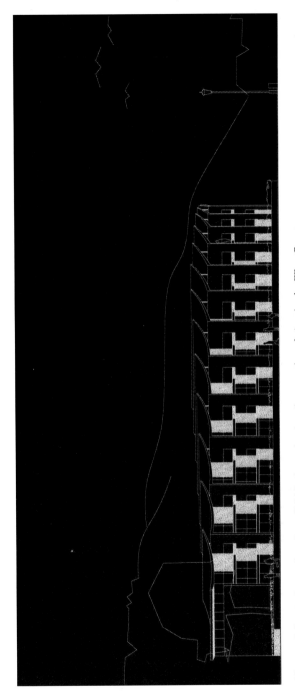

Figure 1.5 Architect Guy Greenfield looks to develop cheap neglected sites in the West Country.

think it's difficult. I have no business skills, really. Like all architects, you have to use your instinct,' says Greenfield, who has formed a partnership with a builder who takes 10 per cent of the profits. 'But you've got to be brave. It's not for the foolhardy.'

Eric Reynolds, director of design and development agency Urban Space Management, says architects should be far more proactive in spotting sites and acting as their own client, especially in inner cities where small, awkward, brownfield plots often evade the attentions of larger developers: 'Maybe your best client is you, and maybe you should be doing the thing yourself and making your own luck.'

Income can also be generated by developing topical specialities (some practices are building up reputations as access specialists, for example, to provide advice on schemes covered by the Disability Discrimination Act). Others market specialist skills as separate brands. Southwark-based Brookes Stacey Randall runs a parallel operation called Brookes Stacey Randall Consultants, which offers specialist cladding advice. In this case, of the 10 employees, eight are capable of acting on behalf of both the architecture practice and the cladding business. The firm was set up in 1987 deliberately as an architecture practice with a specialist consulting arm – partner Michael Stacey completed his Part 3, unusually, while working for a cladding manufacturer. The tactic has been successful because it gives the outfit an extraordinarily wide portfolio of work and is a useful source of short-term income. Although earnings from cladding consulting will never match those of long-term building projects, reasonable sums can be earnt quickly. 'On a £ per hour basis, consultancy work is better; but the overall potential of architecture is probably better,' says Stacey, who recalls advising on the durability of the paint on a new leisure complex in Holland. 'We were well paid for that, but compared with the fee of the architect who designed the building, it would have been very modest.'

☞ **Action points**

• Find a good accountant and make them work hard to provide you with the most tax efficient business model.

- Do your best to maintain a healthy cash flow (see Appendix A).
- Charge the right fee and never feel sorry for your client.
- If fees become the subject of negotiation, point out that fees represent a small part of the overall job.
- Draw up a profit improvement plan. Ask yourself the question: 'What would be the profit effect of an X per cent fee increase, if applied to our top 10 clients?' Then test the water on a sample client.
- Think seriously about becoming your own client and embarking on your own developments (begin small).
- Set up a separate business to market different product ranges/skills. Graphics/visualization businesses offer a good rate of return.
- When bidding for work, work out a realistic assessment of how many hours a job requires. If you make a calculation based on 8-hour days and you then work all night, you are cheating yourself.
- The client interview goes both ways – you are also interviewing them.
- Do not incur overhead costs before you have the work to pay for it.

CASE STUDY – Anthony Hudson Architects

Anthony Hudson's holiday homes venture forms the cornerstone of a strategy to make design pay. As well as giving him the satisfaction of acting as his own client, the venture – Barsham Barns Ltd – was born of a frustration with helping to create large profit margins for clients and getting poorly rewarded in return. The holiday homes business is, he hopes, his pension.

'I think the value architects add to a project is absolutely huge and, although we're not risking our own capital, we clearly miss out on that. To actually benefit from that added value is a huge incentive,' he says. 'But I do see it in the long term. Capital gains tax is a big disincentive to sell, so there's no short-term gain.'

Barsham Barns is a partnership between Hudson and an investment partner from outside the design profession. The company

(a)

(b)

Figure 1.6(a) and (b) Anthony Hudson's award-winning scheme in Norfolk, which launched his development business.

13

has its beginnings in a pair of holiday 'Quaker barns' built by Hudson in Norfolk back in 2001, for which he won a regional RIBA award. These conversions, which were funded by remortgaging his own home for an extra £50 000, can generate anything up to £800 a week, depending on the season. The new business, and a plot purchased near Wells in 2003, is part of a plan to capitalize on this experience and build up a portfolio of property across Norfolk that could be rented or sold according to need.

Hudson believes he has found a gap in a holiday homes market characterized by cottage-effect furniture and rose-covered trellises. Hudson is staking his reputation and financial future on the conviction that enough new generation holidaymakers can be lured away from the chintz. His practice will design the homes, but they will be owned and operated by Barsham Barns, which will collect the profit.

The chances are that Hudson and partner will hang on to their new properties for as long as possible, and will sell up only to plug a financial hole. Holiday homes can be a lucrative business (in high season, charges levied for one week can equal one month's rent for a standard long-term let), and the hope is that inevitable price rises over the long term will eventually generate a handsome profit.

'If we find our interest payments begin to rise, I think we'll have to reduce our borrowings by selling. But at the moment it doesn't make sense. We've done the business plan for these barns and we'll make a profit,' says Hudson.

Hudson has limited his financial stake in the venture, although he has transferred the ownership of the original two barns to the company. Most of the total investment is being provided by his investment partner, with the difference being made up from a bank loan. Significantly, Hudson can increase his own stake in the business through investment-in-kind in the form of design services. This is a plausible model provided that Barsham Barns doesn't take up too much of the practice's time and energy. Hudson estimates the work currently occupies something like 'a sixth to a fifth' of the practice's resources.

The benefits to the practice are clear – the venture guarantees work and the client (being Hudson) will always be sensitive to the design agenda. The practice will be paid costs, and Hudson is developing a sliding fee scale to take account of what the practice needs: the practice could forgo fees and in return increase its stake in Barsham Barns. Alternatively, fees could be paid to make up a shortfall or see a cash flow crisis through.

This architect–client relationship also frees the practice from having to produce a full set of comprehensive drawings. There are drawings, of course, but many of them have not been fully worked out – Hudson will even go on site with a clutch of sketches. 'It's all up here,' he says, tapping his head. 'I run these projects completely differently from the way I would normally run one.'

The price for this relaxed approach is having to spend a lot longer on site, but Hudson enjoys it. Working with local builders, he aspires to the relationship that architects once had with master builders – where the vision of one could, through consultation, be realized through the craft of the other. To enable this to happen, Hudson talks about a 'tolerant' architecture that allows for quick changes of mind, decisions to be taken on the hoof, and one which does not demand exactitude from the contractor. Hudson is the first to admit that, ordinarily, he would instruct a builder to reverse a mistake. However, now that cost-control is just as important as design, Hudson will endeavour to integrate errors into the final build.

CASE STUDY – Lifschutz Davidson

Alex Lifschutz, founding partner of Lifschutz Davidson, believes there is 'too much architecture' being produced in the UK – not only is there too much pressure to produce 'iconic' buildings, but even smaller projects are often designed as one-offs. The result is that many practices spend vast amounts of time, energy and money designing things that needn't be designed at all. And too often this work does not see the light of day as a completed scheme.

Lifschutz sees the answer in product design, that is, architectural systems which can be mass-produced and assembled as a kit of parts. 'I think every project provides an opportunity for a product. The problem for our industry is that every project is seen as an opportunity for wasted design,' he says.

The practice launched its first foray into product design in 1999 when it was appointed to reinvent a 1100 m stretch of uninviting road near London's South Bank. Lifschutz wanted more than just new street lighting, so he set about working with manufacturer Woodhouse to develop a lighting system which doubled up as objects from which to hang large banners – the designs for which were generated via an art competition. This piece of work led to a positive relationship with Woodhouse. Lifschutz Davidson then approached the firm with the idea of developing a catalogue range of street furniture, eventually called Geo. The range, which includes benches, low-level lighting, railings and bicycle racks, is constantly being expanded – a bus shelter is a late addition.

This is not a venture the practice publicizes, but royalties are reasonable. Lifschutz says 'several thousands of pounds' flow into the practice every quarter – not enough to make a major difference, but a regular unexpected bonus. And apart from the money, product design brings further benefits to the office: it forces architects to consider production processes, cost and market demand. 'It does add an extra layer of discipline to your thinking,' says Lifschutz.

This experience and Lifschutz's own research interests (based on the idea that a combination of simple components can result in forms of immense complexity), has encouraged the practice to become more ambitious. It has now developed a component system for constructing apartments with property firm FPD Savilles, as well as a floor system, developed with Arup, which could have a major impact on the design of office/apartment blocks. The 'Truss-floor' system, for example, provides a way of freeing developers from having to make difficult decisions about whether to build an office block or a residential scheme: offices need floor-to-ceiling heights of 3.8 m, while residential units require a minimum of 2.7 m. This makes it almost impossible to convert flats into offices, while converting offices into flats (with generous ceiling heights) is a waste of lettable space. The practice's Truss-floor system, however, provides a way of reaching a compromise by slotting a fully serviced floor into a standard 3.3 m storey. This patented system could, if it becomes widely adopted, earn Lifschutz Davidson and Arup handsome royalties and make new buildings simple to convert from one use to another.

The 'Concept Housing' system for FPD Savilles takes its cue from the automotive and computing industries, which manufacture products with a range of specifications, spanning everything from basic to high-performance models. The system, which can work with the Truss-floors, offers a range of apartment fit-outs for a shell and core development which could be ordered from a catalogue and upgraded by specifying new parts. Designs which cater for different lifestyles, ages and incomes have already been worked out, so individual preferences can be accommodated within the system of standard, quality-controlled units. Also, maintenance contracts could be included in the price, in the same way as a car is purchased with servicing agreements and guarantees.

If the Truss-floor and Concept House become widely accepted building products, the financial benefits are potentially huge, and a serious contribution will have been made to moving construction methods closer to those of the automotive industry. 'With the Truss-floor, Geo and Concept Housing, we could change the way cities are made,' says Lifschutz.

CASE STUDY – Hawkins\Brown

Hawkins\Brown has set up a business which might actually generate revenue from the often thankless job of local community consultation. The idea is to do the job so well that people will want to pay for it. When Lambeth Council ran a competition to find a new use for the derelict Rising Sun pub, Hawkins\Brown won the competition after refusing to design a scheme for the site. Instead, the practice proposed to embark on a major, highly structured consultation process with local people.

Hawkins\Brown has formed a joint venture with the Centre for Social Action, a research and training consultancy affiliated to the University of East Anglia. The joint venture, called Equalise, provides both the architects and the social researchers with a ready-made vehicle for collaboration: they have a name, a brand and a brochure. Better than that, it's an income stream.

Russell Brown complains that most clients expect consultation measures to be undertaken as a matter of course. It is, therefore, underfunded and a matter of doing the bare minimum. When done badly, local people quickly develop 'consultation fatigue' and lose interest. By separating consultation from the design process, resources can be focused on really getting inside the collective mind of a local community – and it becomes an entirely separate, billable piece of work.

'We believe consultation is important and should be properly resourced. It's not just an altruistic thing. This ultimately means we'll get paid for it,' says Brown. Ordinarily, he says, clients abuse practices by expecting them to absorb consultation costs, which explains why it tends to be done on the cheap. 'By setting up Equalise it forces us to think about it more seriously, to consider consultation as research,' he says.

Importantly, Equalise never asks people what they want – if you do that, you end up with a list of impossible dreams which pleases nobody. 'This is one of the golden rules,' says CSA managing director Mark Harrison. 'Asking people what they want is a completely stupid question. All you get is a wish list . . . what people want and what people need are very, very different things.'

Instead, Equalise begins with more focused questions to key residents: What's wrong with your community? What's right with it? Why do you live here? What would you do to improve it? The theory is that people are their own experts in the way they live. Harrison says this forces the professionals, in both the social work and architectural arenas, to do the listening.

This allows ideas to evolve, after which a brief slowly emerges. Only then does the consultation move on to design specifics. This approach has been used with great success to determine the brief and design of a £300 000 young person's drop-in centre in Newham, east London, as well as the £6 million National Centre for Carnival Arts in Luton. The same methodology was used to tackle the problem of the Rising Sun, with the addition that local community groups were asked to submit their ideas to a competition. When the winning scheme is selected, the process will move into the design phase; but having kick-started it, Hawkins\Brown cannot be sure of landing the design work, which already has a £12 million price tag riding on it. They just hope they do.

Importantly, though, effective consultation should add to the practice's stock of successful projects through longevity alone. In other words, it is pointless designing a fabulous public amenity if it soon undergoes a dramatic change of use – or, worse still, is pulled down.

CHAPTER TWO

Marketing

John Durance, chairman of 120-year-old practice Ruddle Wilkinson, says the word 'marketing' is 'hardly in the vocabulary of architects'. He's right and it is a cause for concern among many industry commentators, including the RIBA. Most architects are victims of the myth that the quality of their work is their best marketing tool. Good work is, of course, crucial to the success of any practice, but it is of little use if no one has heard of it.

Part of the problem is that many architects are curiously uncommercial, and consider that the art of their profession ought not be sullied by the dirty act of actually marketing it. But running an architecture practice as a viable business requires the use of any number of commercial tools. In fact, even medium-sized jobs like school extensions, which might very well have gone automatically to a small local practice a few years ago, is now very likely to be awarded to a higher profile practice elsewhere in the country.

Peter Murray – who trained as an architect and has spent most of his career writing on the subject – says it is no coincidence that the UK's most successful practitioners (Norman Foster, Richard Rogers, Nicholas Grimshaw) were knocking on the doors of the architectural magazines 30 years ago. 'Your best marketing is your product, but you have to make sure people know about it. Marketing is a tool to help you fulfil your aims,' he says.

Marketing tools vary considerably, and include all manner of tactics covering public and media relations, business development, publishing, websites, competition entries and client liaison. Importantly, marketing is not all about printing brochures and direct mail. In fact, plenty of practices waste considerable sums in badly thought-out quick fixes. Employing an expensive PR agency to write press releases is no guarantee of media coverage. Equally, pricey monographs run the danger of being nothing more than vanity exercises – the best monographs are those with a distinct message, like Allford Hall Monaghan Morris's *Manual*, which combines the practice's catalogue of work with analysis of how this foursome have gone about building up a business. Anglo-American firm Anshen Dyer has also considered producing a monograph in the form of a series of essays on healthcare design. Hawkins\Brown's book *&\also* (published by Black Dog Publishing in 2003), provides a useful overview of the firm's work along with colourful graphics, punchy essays and challenging (slightly baffling) little statements. For example:

> we are not architects;
> a job title is a red herring;
> something to hide behind;
> like a grey suit;
> better be who we really are;
> people who design buildings;
> letting style follow purpose;
> bin the ego;
> and the letters after the name;
> and the business card that says architect.

In 2003, Peter Murray's communications agency Wordsearch conducted a research exercise into the marketing habits of the UK's larger practices and found that they spend an average of 4 per cent of turnover on marketing. Some spend considerably more, while others spend almost nothing. Moreover, there appears to be a wide variation in who actually undertakes the marketing role in practices. Just over half of those surveyed reported that there was someone tackling marketing as a full-time job, but half of those tend to be architects who have switched roles late in their careers, most of whom have not bothered to get themselves a qualification in the subject. Like most business skills in the profession, which are given scant attention in architecture school, they make it up as they go along.

In truth, the detail of who performs a marketing role and how they go about it is less important than the recognition that focused promotional activity of some sort is a vital part of any business plan. There needs to be a vision shared by everyone who works in the practice – one that is championed by a senior partner and which answers fundamental questions such as: Who are we? What do we want to do? Who are our clients? What are our strengths? and, How do we best communicate our message? The answers should be brought together into a coherent plan for business development, rather than remembered in spare moments. Ruddle Wilkinson has spent a considerable amount of time and energy attempting this, and John Durance is convinced it's been worth it – in 2001 the practice appointed a full-time marketing manager, and by 2004 business had increased by 150 per cent. 'I don't think that is a coincidence,' says Durance.

Practices also need to be clear about the difference between strategy (where you want to go) and tactics (how you get there). Tactics range from the conventional – press releases, competition entries, lecturing – to the unorthodox. Importantly, you need to be comfortable with how you go about marketing yourself. London-based practice M3, featured as a case study on page 28, has developed a range of tactics which some might regard as the epitome of cheek – without the knowledge of the landowner, they'll pick a site and develop such an eye-catching scheme that press attention is almost inevitable. Occasionally, they have unwittingly trodden on other architects' toes, but this gung-ho, proactive approach has also led to useful meetings with potential clients.

It's also worth remembering that tactics need to be matched with specific outcomes. Teaching, for example, is a good way of

ementing your income and raising your profile within
:ctural circles. It's also a good way of networking and
g future employees – but it's unlikely to lead to many
sions. Competitions are also a mixed blessing: while
one can lead to useful press coverage, competition win-
_ a curious habit of remaining unbuilt. Plenty of architects have given up on competitions and consider them a waste
of time and money.

Media relations is also a mixed bag. Any developer worth the
name will be keeping an eye on the architectural press, so there
is nothing wrong with making overtures to titles like *Building
Design, The Architects Journal* and the *RIBA Journal*. But developers, property agents and clients with large property portfolios
are more likely to read the *Estates Gazette, Property Week* and
Building. Also, specialist titles in other sectors, such as the *Local
Government Chronicle, Pulse*, the *Health Service Journal* and *Supply
Management* should also probably be on your radar.

Public relations is something that can be done either in-house or
by a consultancy. There are just as many compelling reasons for
employing your own full-time marketing executive (who would
cover media and public relations) as there are reasons for hiring a
consultant on a daily basis (see Appendix B). Indeed, it's not
uncommon for consultants to work with a practice for a year or
two, training up an in-house team before handing over the reins.
Consultants can be pricey, though, and you're unlikely to have
much change from £350 for a day's work, so choose carefully and
ask for recommendations. If you don't have anyone to ask, call an
architectural magazine; journalists generally have strong opinions
about PR firms and will be able to name two or three decent
people off the top of their heads. Some are listed at the back of this
book. In return for your money you can expect marketing advice,
press contacts, event management, maybe even a little positive
criticism. Some practices build up close, trusting relationships
with consultants – Laura Iloniemi, who represents practices
including Arup Associates and Chetwood Associates, considers
herself as a business sounding board. But what PR agencies cannot do is guarantee work. All they can do is raise your chances.

Having said that, you may not need a consultant at all – especially if all you want is to grab a few column inches in the architectural press from time to time. If you have a proposal or a completed scheme worth publishing, there's nothing wrong with ad hoc, DIY PR. Write an A4 side of bullet points (with a brief description of the project, in simple language, covering price, size, client and key dates), email it to the newsdesks with a couple of handsome Jpegs and hope for the best. Images should be bright, clear, dynamic and saved at around 350 dpi. Add your contact details and make sure you are available to take a call should the phone ring. Never send your only set of high quality (and expensive) prints unsolicited to any publisher, because they will inevitably get lost. And never ring up to ask why your work was never published – you have no right to be published and your material will have to take its place among the mountain of other electronic and paper-based submissions that drop on editors' desks daily.

Remember that monitoring is a crucial part of good marketing practice. Unfortunately, it is almost impossible to monitor the results of every marketing initiative, but that is not to say practices should allocate a marketing budget blindly. It is worth keeping a record of your marketing activity and trying to plot it, at least roughly, against business activity. Writing for a professional journal may be a time-consuming exercise and is a valid piece of marketeering, but it is hard to put a price on it. It may be that, long after publication, the article prompts a potential client to call. Some initiatives are easier to pin down in terms of return on investment – the cost of employing a PR consultant to write and distribute a press release can be compared with the amount of coverage the release generated. Good consultants employ 'cuttings agencies' to spot every mention their clients receive in the press, and they often estimate how much that coverage would have cost if a client had paid for the equivalent space as advertising. Generally, paying for a press release which leads to a reasonable number of media 'hits' will be considerably cheaper than buying an advert. Often, though, marketing is an act of faith. Many practices now refuse to enter architectural competitions because the investment in time and money so rarely pays off – but it is hard to put a price on these things. Even competition losers are often the result of valuable research and are publishable in their own right. No one can ever know when a promotional activity will hit its target. A press release which generates acres of coverage will not necessarily lead to a single new client. However, the slow accumulation of publicity will lead to an aura of success which will eventually be hard to ignore.

Websites represent a good, although passive, marketing tool. There is now a general assumption that any respectable business will have a site, so a lack of one can reflect badly on a practice.

Web design, like marketing generally, is something that can be done in-house or externally. Larger practices, which often employ dedicated graphics teams, can get away with producing their own sites, but smaller practices can run the risk of appearing amateurish. Indeed, many big and well-established practices – including Grimshaw, Alsop and Chapman Taylor – have engaged the services of external web designers. Consequently, the best websites are the result of considerable investment. A reasonable site will cost at least £10 000, but this is probably less than the price of printing and posting thousands of brochures. In fact, the Chapman Taylor site attracts around 100 visitors a day, which is far in excess of the number of brochure requests.

Chapman Taylor relaunched its site, designed by graphics agency Small Back Room, at the beginning of 2003. The exercise was an interesting one. Prior to the redesign, the practice commissioned a specialist research company, Web Trends UK, to analyse useage of the original site. The company found, for example, that half the site's visitors left before a laborious Flash introduction had downloaded. Once this had been spotted, the practice introduced the ability to skip the introduction, instantly increasing the number of visitors.

Flash is a common tool among web designers because it allows them to design unique and exciting interfaces, but architects need to ensure that slick presentation doesn't obscure their message. It is unlikely that any potential client will provide a commission on the strength of a website alone (that will more likely be done on the basis of reputation or personal recommendation), but the web can provide a useful shortcut for clients to build up a broad picture of a practice. Indeed, websites can provide clients with an impression of the personality of the practice, irrespective of the actual content. The Foster site can be read as 'slick', while Hawkins\Brown's creates an image of a 'fun and funky' firm. Others appear commercial and even banal, especially when information is woefully out of date. David Partridge, architect and deputy chief executive of developer Argent, conducted a review of architects' websites for *Building Design* in 2003. He wrote that he could tell a lot about a practice by the way it put a website together: 'Subliminally the sites were telling me what to expect of the process of actually building a building with these architects. They're a sort of personification of the architects themselves, a window into their soul.'

Any website should contain a short practice declaration or a statement of beliefs and values. Also contact details should be easy to come by, as well as brief descriptions and photographs of completed work. Crucially, site information should not be made available as automatic downloads. Allowing a visitor to source a PDF of a project description is sensible, but this should remain purely optional. Often, networked computers do not allow users to download material from the web, so sites that are configured as a set of downloads can become a source of frustration.

In fact, a practice should draw up a statement of beliefs and values anyway, irrespective of whether or not it appears in promotional campaigns. Just as there is such a thing as internal communications, there is internal marketing. Staff need a well articulated brand/identity/belief system to rally around and it will be easier to market yourself to the public if you already have your staff on side.

☞ Action points

- Identify your target markets and draw up a marketing plan.
- Make sure someone at the practice takes responsibility for marketing.

- Marketing can take many forms (e.g. website, lectures, events, press relations). Make sure you are comfortable with the tactics you choose.
- A practice should ask itself the questions: 'Who are we? What do we do? What can we offer?'
- Publicize success whenever possible. Remember that building projects have many stages at which publicity is appropriate: a competition win, a planning application, planning approval, going on site, nearing completion, completion. But remember, you do not have to try and publicize everything – publicize only the work you are proud of and which reinforces your brand.
- Timing is essential for press coverage. There is no point in delivering, for example, a controversial lecture and sending out the transcript a month later. Press material needs to be sent in advance under a strict embargo date. An embargo is a matter of trust. If you have cultivated good relationships with the press you can be confident an embargo will be respected. If an embargo is broken, protest loudly.
- When dealing with the press, make it clear when you are speaking on and off the record.
- Good images help underpin good marketing. Look at what gets published and what is exhibited, and compare it with your own work.
- Weigh up the pros and cons of in-house PR and using a consultant (see Appendix B). You may even use both.
- Try to convey a strong, individual message in all your marketing activity.

CASE STUDY – M3

Ken Hutt and Nadi Jahangiri set up M3 in May 1997 after working together at Foster & Partners. Setting up on their own was almost inevitable ('It was an itch we had to scratch,' they say), but the pair have not gone about it in a conventional manner. Their business model and the way they go about finding work is highly unusual, but it appears to be paying dividends.

Figure 2.1   M3's tactic of 'project making' leads to unlikely proposals. Here, a parasitic house attaches itself to an office block in London's Old Street . . . .

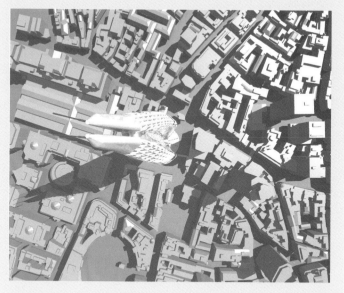

Figure 2.2   . . . and here, an eco-tower rises above the capital.

Figure 2.3 M3fx, M3's visualization arm, provides a useful income stream for the design business.

Both stress that they didn't have any 'posh relatives' to turn to for building commissions when leaving the security of Fosters. When they started out on their own, they had nothing: 'We took the view – what's the worst that can happen? So we began in my front room from a standing start, with no money, no commissions and no work,' says Jahangiri. For the first year Jahangiri stayed at home trying to build up a practice, while Hutt got hold of as much contract work as he could – and they split the money at the end of every month.

Eventually, they gained the confidence to rent 400 square feet of office space in London's Clerkenwell, setting them back a reasonable £4000 in the first year. They stayed for 3 years, during which time they took on staff and hatched their own business model. In fact, there is one model, and three businesses.

Hutt and Jahangiri are accomplished architects with a strong track record – at Fosters they worked on projects including the Commerzbank headquarters in Frankfurt, the Reichstag and Hong Kong's Chek Lap Kok airport. Striking out on their own, the last thing they wanted was to get drawn into loft extensions and garage conversions – they wanted, and still want, to engage in 'challenging' architecture which addresses big issues like sustainability and transport. The trouble is, small, fledgling practices rarely get the chance to tackle these themes, not at any scale anyway. So Hutt and Jahangiri have tried to make their own chances.

They hired an interior designer and a graphics specialist and set up two new divisions – M3 Interiors and M3fx, an architectural graphics and visualization outfit. The interior designer was given an equity share in the new business and a percentage of annual income, while the graphic designer was provided with a basic salary and a profit share guarantee, so both were incentivized to make the ventures work. As it turned out, they did work, and the different divisions now trade as separate business entities rather than as trading units of one company. Hutt and Jahangiri are partners in M3 Architects, set up as a limited liability partnership, and directors of the two other companies, set up as limited companies. The name M3 is now an over-arching brand that unifies these separate enterprises.

There are a number of benefits to this approach. Firstly, the three practices (which employ a total of only eight people) can pull together on a single project when needed, but they can also act independently. And as independent firms, they each provide Hutt and Jahangiri with an income which allows the pair to pursue the kind of architecture they want. Setting up the visualization business was particularly canny – photorealistic renderings are increasingly in demand and M3fx has picked up a good list of clients: Arup Associates, KPF, the Manhattan Loft Corporation and British Airways, among others. Moreover, graphics are quicker to turn around than buildings and provide a relatively good return on time invested ('and they don't leak,' says Hutt).

In fact, this business model has proved so successful that there could be other M3s – Hutt and Jahangiri have already registered the domain names M3 Developments and M3 Projects, just in case they diversify into property development or project management. A further benefit to the approach is that (because they are set up as separate businesses) if any of these ventures goes belly up, it is unlikely to affect the others too badly.

The net result is that M3 Architects can concentrate on what it wants, rather than grabbing everything that comes along. The practice will even turn work away. In fact, in 7 years M3 Architects has, to date, built relatively little – just a handful of smart houses and apartments. But the security of having an income stream from other viable business allows Hutt and Jahangiri to pitch for ambitious work. They describe one of their tactics as 'project making' – essentially, inventing work for themselves.

Project making involves picking a site, drawing up an ambitious solution to its perceived problems and then publishing the results. If a proposal is bright, bold and beautiful enough, most architectural magazines will give it a slot, and this is a useful way of attracting attention to yourself. London's Old Street tube station was one such target – King's Cross railway station was another which, after getting in the *Architects' Journal* and *Building Design*, managed to irritate John McAslan who had already been appointed to draw up a scheme. But it did have the benefit of leading to introductions at London Underground and RailTrack. These imaginative, client-less schemes play a useful marketing role. For the last 4 years, the practice has exhibited its work in the Royal Academy's Summer Show.

The M3 federation now appears to be on a firm footing. Hutt and Jahangiri bought their own office space in the heart of Clerkenwell in 2003 and have fitted it out as a showcase of their work. On present form, the emergence of M3 as a design heavy-weight is only a matter of time.

CASE STUDY – Land TransMedia

In 2003, Land Design Studio, the 10-strong design practice best known for its work on the National Maritime Museum in Falmouth and the Dome's Play Zone, launched a new trading division. The venture is part of a drive to develop new services and enter new markets, and the hope is that this new technology-focused entity will be clearly distinguishable from its older brother, which has established an enviable reputation as a provider of interactive spaces for museums.

The result of the launch is two divisions, each with their own names (Landesign and Land TransMedia), their own business

Figure 2.4 Landesign's concept for a UK pavilion for Expo '05, to be built in Aichi, Japan.

Figure 2.5 The pavilion's interior.

cards and websites. They are each described as trading divisions of Land Design Studio Ltd, and the accounts of each will be clearly demarcated. But (adopting a model similar to that used by M3) each will be staffed by exactly the same people. Land has, in a corporate sense, become schizophrenic. This tactic is based on the idea that well-trained, experienced staff are capable of performing more than just one function. In marketing terms it allows you to pitch yourself as a collection of specialist consultancies, rather than a jack-of-all-trades. It allows you to bid for work that might appear to be outside your normal scope of operations. It also makes you seem bigger than you really are.

Figure 2.6 Landesign's exhibition space for the National Maritime Museum, Cornwall.

Land TransMedia (or Land™) is designed as a marketing tool to 'reposition' the practice and enter new markets – essential, says creative director Peter Higgins, because the large Heritage Lottery Fund grants which underpinned a good deal of Landesign's work are drying up. Much of the practice's work has had a heavy technological bias, and Higgins believes that its research is just as relevant to communications firms, like BT, as it is to the museums and galleries sector.

The idea is to repackage the practice's research and technology expertise and offer it as a specific and separate service, free from the heritage tag that accompanies most of the practice's work: 'In a sense our reputation works against us, if we want to cross the line into corporate design.'

There is also another benefit. Land has long been able to both conceptualize and actually deliver technology and design solutions, but clients are often wary of firms doubling up. Clients often prefer to draw up separate contracts with different specialists. In legal and contract terms, technology specialists Land™ can act as a supplier to architect and interior design firm Landesign. In reality, of course, the practice is acting as a supplier to itself.

'Very rarely do people ask us to do the architecture and to do the technology. In an ideal world I'd like to do the lot,' says Higgins, who spent £70 000 creating a pair of DVDs to explain and market both divisions as separate entities. As this book went to press Land™ was beginning to generate work. Before too long, the two divisions could well be trading in some sort of equilibrium.

CASE STUDY – Piercy Conner

Piercy Conner Architects, set up by Stuart Piercy and Richard Conner after a spell at Grimshaw, were all but unknown until August 2001. But when *The Guardian* carried a front page story describing the practice's 'Microflat' concept, everything changed. Further press coverage attracted the attention of Vittorio Radice, then chief executive of Selfridges, who offered Piercy Conner the chance to build a full-scale Microflat in the window of his Oxford Street store, complete with live occupants dubbed 'micronauts'. The PR stunt led to a Carlton TV documentary watched by 4 million people, coverage in all UK broadsheets, further stories in international newspapers including the *New York Times* and *Suddeutsche Zeitung*, and airtime on *Richard & Judy*. The practice estimates that, if it had actually paid for this coverage, the bill would have topped £4 million.

Actually, the publicity wasn't entirely free. The Selfridges exercise cost £80 000, none of which was covered by the store. The practice's freelance PR consultant Sam Price managed to raise £70 000 from sponsors including Neff and Intel, but the architects had to raise the rest. The investment was worth it. Sam Price went on to win *PR Week*'s Solo Practitioner of the Year Award, and the practice either won or was short-listed for awards by the Institute of Public Relations and the Chartered Institute of Marketing. The team and graphics agency Smoothe (set up by Piercy Conner as a separate income stream) have since been asked to join a BBC think tank set up to generate documentary ideas.

Figure 2.7   Piercy Conner's Microflat concept.

Figure 2.8 In spite of slick imagery, the Microflat is still awaiting a real site.

The Microflat was a simple idea. Based on the compactness of yacht interiors, Piercy Conner devised a 33-m^2 living module that was affordable, flexible, prefabricated, attractive and small enough to be erected in any number of configurations on unwanted inner-city sites. The name also helped. Cleverly, the practice has

Figure 2.9 The Microflat, and its exhibition at Selfridge's, netted Piercy Conner £4 million worth of free advertising.

trademarked the name and registered The Microflat Company as a separate business which, with a FTSE 250 investment company, will manage the sale of the flats. The company website has attracted more than 75 000 visitors and 2700 people have registered for a flat. All the practice needs to do now is secure planning permission, and negotiations were advanced with one London borough in mid-2004.

'You've got to hand it to them. The publicity garnered by the Microflat concept . . . is immense. Building a real one in the corner of Selfridges, with real live Micronauts living there for a week at a time, is a PR idea bordering on genius,' wrote Hugh Pearman in *The Sunday Times*.

CHAPTER THREE

Staying small

Most British architectural practices are small. Just over half have less than 10 employees, and only a quarter of practices are staffed by more than 30 people. A good many architects, around 20 per cent, practice on their own.

It is important to understand that running a small practice is not a sign of failure; indeed, many architects have ambitions to stay small. Staying small allows an architect to keep a firm grip on the creative process, to respond quickly to client demand and to remain free of the inevitable administrative burden of employing large numbers of staff. Some small practices appear to be slightly embarrassed by their size, and it is not uncommon to find sole practitioners adding the suffix '& Associates' to their name in an effort to make themselves appear bigger. Other practices have been known to bring in students to swell numbers when an important client is to visit the office, and practices which share spaces with other creative companies rarely disabuse visitors of the impression that they are looking at a single firm.

It is true that many clients might be wary of awarding a significant commission to a small practice, for the simple reason that they believe large budgets are best handled by large firms. This is not always the case though. Developer Derwent Valley prides itself on championing small, innovative and creative practices; so does Peabody Housing Trust. But if size really is a genuine client concern, it's handy having a few examples up your sleeve which prove precisely the opposite: the international competition to build a national museum overlooking the pyramids of Giza was won, for example, by the relatively unknown Dublin duo Heneghan Peng. As this book went to press, the five-strong New Forest practice John Pardey Architects was steering a £10 million housing project through the planning system. And the masterplan for Wood Wharf, an extension to the Canary Wharf business district, was put together by a pair of sole practitioners, Nick Kuhn and Jonathan Reeves (see Figure 6.1).

Many practices simply don't want to grow, preferring to maintain an informal studio atmosphere. Some architects even make the semantic distinction between a 'studio' and a 'business', although there is little agreement about where the threshold lies.

Some small practices, though, just aren't big enough. Bath-based Aaron Evans Architects, which employs 10 people, is at the limit of what most commentators would define as 'small'. But limited growth is on the cards because Evans believes he hasn't quite got the 'critical mass' to attract the big-budget jobs he wants. Although the practice has managed to land a handful of reasonably large contracts, including a £10.5 million cinema complex in the centre of Bath, Evans is concerned that the arrival and completion of big projects causes unhealthy swings in staffing levels. 'We enjoyed a long period when we were under 10 people, which was great for a while. But it comes at a cost. When a job we really wanted came along, we had to grow rapidly and suddenly. It was a strain,' says Evans, who set up on his own in 1978 and gave himself just 6 months to make it. Evans wants the practice to grow to something nearer 20 people, which he believes will give him the capacity to soak up large new projects without radically altering his workforce. 'I don't necessarily want to grow much larger than that, but I figure that at that size we'll have the flexibility we need. It will also allow us to increase our investment in research and training.'

Whatever the size of the business, there is nothing to absolve small practitioners from the responsibilities of running a sound business – you still need an accountant and an office manager (if you grow to more than four people, a part-time office manager will probably become a necessity). You still need a marketing plan and efficient administration systems. Fortunately, there are now plenty of software options which provide a good alternative to stuffing paperwork in shoeboxes. Off-the-shelf software which brings together every single aspect of an architect's professional life (design, email, archiving, word processing, resourcing, payroll, etc.) has yet to be invented, but some software houses have made a good start. Fido software's program autotrac-architect looks like such a convincing attempt to wrap up these functions that most of the business affairs of entire practices could be carried around in a laptop. Software developer Union Square provides similar, highly regarded products. And for accounting, nobody would call you a fool for purchasing Sage, an accounts and business tool designed especially for small- and medium-sized enterprises. Unfortunately, Sage is not configured for Macs, but the program MYOB makes a perfectly good alternative (see Appendix F).

Running a small practice requires a specific kind of personality. You need to thrive on facing the unknown and must have a genuine conviction that you don't want to work for anyone else. The chances are, by running a reasonably successful small practice, an architect will earn more than they would as a salaried employee – but you have to work a lot harder for it. And it's worth remembering that, should the business fail or you simply cannot put up with the stress of an uncertain financial future any longer, getting a job as a salaried employee might not be an option. There are directors of large practices who would not offer a job to someone who had been running their own show for too long. By setting up on their own, architects often make themselves unemployable. 'When you're running a very small business, you do need a certain approach to life. You can't panic too soon and you need to have enough give and take to let things go,' says sole practitioner Simon Foxell.

From a client point of view, there are natural advantages to dealing with a small practice. Clients can usually be guaranteed that the practice director will very likely handle their design work, while the *esprit de corps* fostered among the staff of a small practice is second to none. And by harnessing the potential of IT, firms with just a handful of employees (M3, Piercy Conner, Land, Softroom) can produce award-winning work of unparalleled creativity. However, recent years have thrown a number of obstacles in the way of small firms: the advent of the Private Finance Initiative (PFI), framework agreements (see Appendix C) and the fact that local authorities are now bound to seek 'best value' in all their purchases (meaning that they often look further than their own local communities for architects) are not good news for small practices. Very large contractors and multidisciplinary practices can offer economies of scale that squeeze small practices out of the market. Apart from that, the paperwork required by an application is immense and can swamp even the biggest firms. When a county council wants to commission a dozen new schools, a five-person practice is unlikely to be shortlisted even if it wanted the work.

There are exceptions, though, such as Jordan & Bateman Architects which has signed a framework agreement with the Foreign and Commonwealth Office, along with much larger firms like HOK International, GMW and TPS Consult. Framework agreements contain no in-built prejudice against small practices so long as they can demonstrate unequivocally that they can offer a good track record of relevant work. Jordan & Bateman was fortunate, then, that partner John Bateman had worked at the Foreign Office during the 1980s. After setting up the practice in 1991, he went on to win a number of prestigious jobs for his former employer – including a consular building in Ghana, a complex in Chennai (Madras) and a residence for new embassy staff in Pyong Yang. This stood him in good stead when applying for the framework agreement in 2001, via an Ojec notice that attracted nearly 300 expressions of interest. It is harder to find a better example of the efficacy of John McAslan's advice at the beginning of this book: 'Build relationships – you never know who you might need in the future.'

In the main, however, small practices are finding it more difficult to obtain the larger, reputation-building jobs that were once easier to come by. A leaflet published by the RIBA in 2003, *Best Practice Small Practice*, is highly critical of this development: 'Fortunately, we do not yet require our novels or paintings to be created by large companies but, as with design, we would be the poorer if we did.'

The answer to this conundrum probably lies in collaboration. The Acanthus network, set up by George Ferguson in 1986, allows its dozen members of medium-sized practices to punch above their weight by sharing a national brand and providing a forum for ideas, benchmarking and even job sharing. Ferguson's practice, Bristol-based Acanthus Ferguson Mann, numbers around 30 staff which makes it one of the largest members of the group (with 200 staff in total, the average size of an Acanthus practice is 17). But all have an equal voice. Although each practice remains independent, they each nominate a director to sit on the board of Acanthus Associated Architectural Practice Ltd, the company which provides the formal focus of the network. The company has a bank account, into which every member deposits an annual sum based on head count. The chairman of the board rotates annually.

The benefit of Acanthus is that it is deliberately composed of practices around the country, which adds a 'local' flavour to the national reach. Also, it reduces the danger of members competing against each other for jobs. If collaboration is required in order to secure a contract, it is unlikely that member practices will combine design teams (something which Ferguson is convinced would be a 'real struggle'), but members often pool their expertise and act as consultants to each other. This means that members can pitch for jobs which, without the back up of Acanthus, they would be unqualified.

Architect Hugo Tugman seems to have figured out a way of using networking to make a profit from low-budget domestic jobs, traditionally the meat and drink of small practice. RIBA figures show that domestic work is by far the biggest building sector undertaken by practices of less than 10 people. The trouble is, architects often struggle to make much, if any, profit out of budgets of less than £50 000, so they either turn them down or take the work reluctantly. Tugman's network, architect-yourhome, seems to have found a way around this problem. Architectyourhome, set up in 2002, is a web-based service that allows clients to select (and pay for) as many or as few of an architect's services as they like, in any combination, and their query gets forwarded to a local member practice. Furthermore, marketing and billing functions are provided centrally, and every job is handled by a central account manager. Member practices, and there were 14 by mid-2004, are not obliged to take the work, but Tugman insists that every job is profitable. By itemizing everything, charging a decent hourly rate, insisting that clients pay by debit card and freeing the practices from having to chase bills, Tugman's model is certainly an attractive one.

☞ Action points

- Small practices should network and share information. Many small firms actually enjoy benchmarking themselves against each other and honestly exchange information with their peers (especially on matters such as salaries, fees, pitches/jobs won, administration solutions).
- Some clients do have a problem with giving work to small practices. Formal networks, where practices share resources/offices/skills can help you present yourself as a much larger business.
- Decide what work you want to do and, when the time is right, begin to turn down work that gets in the way of your ambitions.
- In your promotional material, point out that all clients will benefit from dealing with the practice director.
- Even though you are small, do not underestimate the amount of administration required to make a business run efficiently – even

one with an annual turnover as small as £100 000. Invest in the right software (see Appendix F).

- Very small practices need not inhabit rented accommodation – a room in the director's home may be sufficient. Client meetings can take place anywhere, and many sole practitioners never conduct meetings in their office. Do not incur the overhead of renting/buying a dedicated office space unless it is necessary (e.g. you intend to grow or if you want to use your office as a showcase for your work).
- Overheads can be reduced by sharing office space. Sharing with other creative businesses (graphic designers, new media, product designers) can lead to opportunities for collaboration. Apart from that, it makes your business look bigger.
- Establish links with key strategic players in your area – find out who has the architecture brief in your Regional Development Agency and build a rapport with your architecture centre (if you have one). Use the plentiful opportunities provided by the RIBA branch network.
- Be aware of local politics. Impending council elections may have an effect on a planning application, especially if the local press have a view on a potential building scheme.
- Take a few calculated risks. Remember the advice given to architect John Pardey by a businessman client (see below): 'If you're scared, you won't do anything.' Alternatively, there's the quote by author M.H. Alderson: 'If at first you don't succeed, you are running about average.'

CASE STUDY – Forster Inc.

Rachel and Jonathan Forster set up design practice Forster Inc. in 1998. The practice is unusual in that the two partners are siblings, but their close interests (and the fact that their family relationship means that no one is likely to run off with the firm's assets) makes for a firm of particular strength. Both are graduates of the Royal College of Art, Jonathan in furniture design (1995) and Rachel in architecture and interior design (1997). Their collaboration began after securing a £12 000 job for a hairdressing academy in London's Shoreditch. At about the same time, they qualified for a £2500 loan from the Prince's Youth Trust and an identical sum from the bank.

Since then, the pair have managed to carve out a healthy living by staying small. They have no permanent employees, but can call on a wide network of other professionals – covering design, project management, engineering, graphics, surveying and contracting – to enable them to tackle jobs of considerable complexity and size. Generally, the value of Forster Inc's projects ranges between £20 000 and £250 000, but Rachel Forster is confident of taking on projects worth at least half a million. Broadly speaking, the practice charges a fee beginning at around 20 per cent of the contract value for small jobs – the percentage shrinks as budgets increase.

Although growth, in terms of employees, is the subject of 'constant discussion', Rachel Forster insists the main attraction of staying small is the sense of control that accrues from limited size. The Forsters feel in total command of their work because they have the time and opportunity to take a close interest in every stage of a project. The practice expands and contracts to deal with the work load, but the pair always have close control over the end product. Clients commission the practice in the certain knowledge that every last detail will be designed and overseen by the individuals who actually pitched for the work. Moreover, the absence of permanent staff keeps overheads down.

'We wouldn't say no to bigger projects. We could definitely handle them efficiently because we've got the back up of freelance designers and consultants,' says Rachel Forster, who has around 10 jobs, in varying stages of completion, on the go at any one time.

She adds that a further benefit of remaining small, however, is that it provides the opportunity to take on interesting, slightly curious, microscale work that larger practices would probably ignore – such as pet shops and estate agents. 'We like getting into areas that haven't really been designed before.' Even very small jobs are worth pursuing. The practice once took on a £12 000 job to design an elaborate shelving unit. This intelligent piece of work subsequently led to further commissions.

Staying small, in numbers if not in outlook, also provides the room to explore other income streams and take marketing seriously. As a former shop, the front of the practice's office lends itself to use as an exhibition space, providing an opportunity for Forster Inc. to demo its own work (other designers showing their products hand over a percentage of any sales). The practice also makes a point of collaborating in the design festival that accompanies the annual 100% Design exhibition. 'For us it's an opportunity to be part of a larger event and promote ourselves under the umbrella of a recognized brand,' says Rachel Forster.

Each year the practice uses 100% to exhibit a speculative design project. In 2003, they tackled urban design with the project 'The City of Shoreditch', which proposed a visionary plan for this tough corner of London. The project introduced the Forsters to urban design, an area they are keen to break into, and provided an opportunity to collaborate with other design and communication disciplines.

'Successful marketing is about reaching the right audience and letting them know what you are about. Involvement in events has built our profile and enabled us to reach an audience beyond our immediate circle of contacts. The indirect nature of this marketing, where we can present and talk about our work, is enjoyable and complements other more direct approaches,' says Rachel Forster.

This is the beauty of a small practice: thorough, nimble, responsive, entrepreneurial, taking opportunities where they can be found.

CASE STUDY – John Pardey Architects

John Pardey set up his own practice in the late 1980s and has adopted two strategies that, at first sight, appear to make little business sense. First, he intends to remain as a 'studio practice' rather than a 'business'; and second, he turns plenty of work away that doesn't suit him.

Figure 3.1 John Pardey rarely accepts work worth less than £300, 000.

Figure 3.2 Pardey refuses to work for 'banal' developers, prefering to design buildings with 'soul'.

This is a model that works. For most of the last 16 years he has practised on his own, with the help of the occasional student assistant, but he now employs four architects and has 20 jobs at varying stages of completion, including a house for the BBC's head of drama. Most of the practice's work is focused on the housing and education sectors, and Pardey rarely accepts anything with a build cost of less than £300 000. Roughly once a week he

Figure 3.3 'We're trying to do really good stuff, here. A one-off house is great,' says Pardey.

turns a potential client down, mainly because the budget is too small for him to design anything that will give him job satisfaction. Also, he tends not to work for 'banal' developers.

This 'all or nothing' approach to business is the result of a firm conviction that the only point in studying architecture is to secure the opportunity to undertake high quality, intellectually stimulating buildings with 'soul'. He found the courage to do what he wants after a former client, a successful businessman, told him 'if you're scared, you won't do anything'.

'It sounds snobbish, but we're trying to do really good stuff here. A one-off house is great. It's not about the money, it's about clients who can provide the minimal level of investment to do something that will endure,' says Pardey, who adds that very small projects 'just weigh you down.'

Success for this New Forest-based practice has not come easily. Although he has won around 20 architectural competitions, only one has ended up being built. Teaching at Portsmouth University 'provided a rudder that kept me going', he admits. His fortunes began to turn in 2000 when he extended and renovated a house designed by Sir Basil Spence in 1961 – a project for which he won a RIBA award and received coverage in the *Architects Journal*. Since then Pardey has secured more lucrative commissions, moved to larger premises and taken on permanent staff. The chances are that he will grow even further, but Pardey is adamant that there is a limit to expansion. The last thing he wants is for his practice to become so large that he spends more time running the business than designing. Neither does he want the stress of what he calls 'just running a business'.

'There is a limit, although I don't know where it is – somewhere between 10 and 20 people,' he says. 'There is a difference between a business and a studio practice. I see myself very much as a studio. It's hard work, but very informal.'

CASE STUDY – Stan Bolt

Like John Pardey, Stan Bolt turns down work in order to concentrate on contemporary, domestic design – he also concentrates on wealthy/enlightened clients based in the south-west who require schemes in spectacular settings. And apart from restricting himself stylistically, Bolt has set himself a very definite geographical horizon. Based in Brixham, Devon, he refuses to work outside a 2-hour drive from his office. This gives him a field of operations stretching from mid-Cornwall to Dorset. Carving out such a niche market has worked out well, and Bolt has won a string of RIBA and Civic Trust awards, as well as coverage in the national press.

'There aren't many practices around here that do what we do – a crisp, contemporary style,' said Bolt, adding that the local landscape provides contexts that city-based architects can only dream about. 'The environment is inspiring itself. When you go on site, it's a beach and you can have a swim afterwards. It's a different way of life.'

Bolt insists he has 'no desire whatsoever' to grow into a large practice. He employs three architects and is unlikely to get much bigger. When he set up on his own, Bolt set himself some stretching (even idealistic) parameters. Significantly, he turned his back on the work that most young practices would consider their staple diet.

Figure 3.4 Stan Bolt restricts himself to one-off projects in stunning locations.

'Roof extensions just beget more roof extensions; garage conversions just beget more garage conversions. I didn't study architecture to do that,' he said. 'I'd rather sell ice creams on the beach than do garage conversions. But it has been tough. At first I did struggle financially.'

Figure 3.5 'Roof extensions just beget more roof extensions,' says Bolt.

Figure 3.6 Based in the south-west, Bolt rarely works beyond a two-hour drive from his office.

CHAPTER FOUR

Managing growth

A definition of a large practice is hard to come by. For John Pardey the limit is around 20 people. Joanna van Heyningen would not want to top 30. Alex Lifschutz, of Lifschutz Davidson, has ambitions to grow from 45 to around 60, which would have qualified as a very large practice a decade or two ago. Geoff Mann, a director of RHWL, is comfortable keeping numbers at around 150. On a practice by practice basis, these figures seem reasonable, but it is probably unwise to declare a limit to expansion. If a client turns up with a dream project which demands taking on staff, most architects will grab their chance. But growth, and its consequences, requires careful management.

Whether expansion has been the result of planning (like the 800-strong Aedas) or accident (the 170-strong Allies & Morrison), practice leaders must take stock and reinvent the corporate hierarchy. Once a practice goes beyond 30 people, it becomes impossible for partners/directors to carry resourcing information around in their heads. There is no single model for running a practice of this size. But there is a spectrum along which firms sit, ranging from those where the practice is essentially an extension of the founder (like Zaha Hadid or David Chipperfield) to those where the founder becomes a support mechanism for everybody else.

In black and white terms, the choice is this: design or administration. Unless you want to become a full-time manager and keep only a passing interest in design work, architects need to hand the responsibility for day-to-day administrative matters over to specialist staff. Founders of most large practices occupy the middle ground – specialists are employed to handle technical issues like office management, human resources, marketing and IT, leaving directors to look for new business, handle clients and oversee design output at a strategic level, via regular design reviews and corporate crits. It is not uncommon to meet directors of large practices who spend no more than 25 per cent of their time on design-related matters. The trick is nurturing dependable staff who complement directors, and delegating responsibility for everyday design work.

Inevitably, there are some radical and commercially sound exceptions. Arup Associates, for example, abandoned its pyramidal management structure in 2001 and replaced it with a board of 14 'practice principals' – architects and engineers who run the practice collectively until they reach the age of 58, when they step down and resume their careers as full-time designers. Helped by three forums (covering strategy, operations and new business) the principals see themselves as temporary guardians of the practice, rather than its owners. Moreover, principals spend a good deal of their time running their own projects and submitting their team's design work to tough, very public, crits by a Design Review Panel. Life at Arup Associates can be hard, but it is extremely fair. This is no place for ego, and younger staff appreciate the egalitarianism of the office and the fact that the age limit for principals opens up a career path.

This co-operative approach has similarities with the way multidisciplinary design practice Pentagram runs its affairs. Again, the practice does not have a single voice. There is no chairman or managing director – nor has there ever been. Instead, the practice is run by equal partners who manage their own affairs, recruit their own staff, bring in their own work and pool their earnings. The ethos that has built up over three decades is that work should be interesting and fun, and that the promise of hefty fees should not be the prime reason to take a job on. As long as they pull their weight, produce justifiable design solutions and are committed to the idea of learning from one another, partners can plough their own furrow. And one partner gets paid the same as any other.

'When partners come to work, they worry about their work, not the business. Pentagram is a platform from which you take new steps,' Daniel Weil, Pentagram partner, told FX magazine. 'There is no corporate view that will force the hand of anybody. When we judge a principal's work, we judge it according to their discipline's needs.'

This idealistic arrangement is spectacularly successful. From the original five partners the practice has grown to encompass 19 partners and around 150 staff. The London office has also spawned equally viable outposts in New York, San Francisco and Austin, Texas. Moreover, Pentagram has managed to outlive all its founders, four of whom have retired, while architect Theo Crosby died in 1994. Careful selection of new faces means that the collegiate ethos is as strong as ever.

This is probably not a model that can be applied universally, however. The danger with flat management structures is that decision-making can be slow and frustrating, and there is less clarity about where the buck stops. Also, practices which operate in this way need to recruit/coach a special breed of person, someone who is competitive enough to make it to the top table, but restrained enough to resist the temptation to dominate. For most practices a traditional pyramidal hierarchy provides a structure which, as well as fostering both stability and certainty, can survive periods of growth and contraction relatively intact. The whole point of a hierarchy is simple: it is there to facilitate the efficient running of the business, not to indulge the ambitions of individuals. The further up the hierarchy one moves, the more strategic the role. Terminology may vary but, broadly, this means installing a board of directors, including a chairman and chief executive. There may even be a non-executive director or two, someone from outside the industry who is recruited to provide advice rather than assume management responsibilities.

Ideally, each director will assume responsibility for a specific issue (HR, IT, etc.) to which full-time specialist managers will report. Well-qualified, non-architectural support staff, like HR (which covers functions like payroll, recruitment, employment policy, training and equal opportunities) might well be taken on at fairly senior level, especially if these employees are to be given some sort of strategic voice. Also, architects must realize that there comes a time when non-architects should be promoted to the very top of the business – an accountant is an obvious choice, although there are strong arguments for reserving a board seat for a marketing/business development professional. This is common practice in general industry, but is extremely rare in the architectural profession. Beneath the board there will be a series of management layers: non-board directors, senior managers/associates, associates and so on.

This is a model that has served Aedas well. Aedas, with more than 800 staff in offices around the UK and the Far East, is now one of the largest practices in the world. This has been a deliberate policy of survival through expansion and diversification, effected through a handful of mergers, since the late 1990s. When director Peter Oborn joined the practice, then called Abbey Hanson Rowe, there were already 175 employees, a figure which grew to 300 after the merger with Holford Associates a decade later in 1999 (when the partnership converted to a limited company). Numbers were further boosted when the practice merged with Temple Cox Nichols in 2002. The practice now employs around 500 people in nine offices across the UK, each of which is a profit centre. A strategic alliance forged with Hong Kong-based Liang Peddle Thorp, which led to the creation of the Aedas brand, has propelled the practice into the world top 10. Inevitably, for a practice of this size, PFI jobs and framework

Figure 4.1 Aedas's concept for a new inner-city education centre.

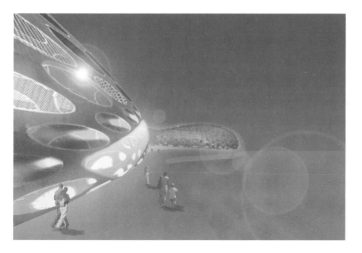

Figure 4.2 The new Aedas Studio, led by Richard Hyams, has been conceived to 'push the boat out'.

agreements provide a significant proportion of the firm's income. Turnover and profit are up. 'Certainly in the UK there is no part of the business that hasn't benefited from what we have done,' says Oborn.

Figure 4.3 Bizarre forms are becoming part of the usual design exploration process at Aedas.

Crucially, the practice doesn't 'feel' like a very large business because of its regional spread. Each office, including the one in London, seats 50–100 people. But in spite of the number of offices, the practice has drawn up a very tight, effective corporate hierarchy, consisting of 23 equity-holding directors, of whom eight form the company board, followed by (non-equity) regional directors, associate directors and associates. A central management team, based in Huddersfield, comprises specialist HR, IT, marketing and production staff. Importantly, every function and every office has director-level representation, which feeds into a board headed up by a chairman and a chief executive. And, in order to make sure design quality is not forgotten, the practice recruited Richard Hyams from Foster & Partners in 2003 to fill the post of design director and spearhead a new initiative, called Aedas Studio, to 'push the boat out' and improve the standard and consistency of design throughout the practice.

As this book went to press, Aedas directors were actively considering raising the profile of non-architectural roles and allowing the possibility of admitting, for example, marketing and

HR professionals to director level. 'If these functions are to provide the level of added value we want, then they should have director-level status,' says Oborn, who adds that this move is part of the practice 'growing up'.

Cleverly, Aedas seems to have struck a good balance between devolution and central planning. It has all the benefits of being a large national practice without the cost of running a giant London office, and it has the advantages of regional spread without being dismissed as 'provincial'.

There is an alternative to massive growth, though. Collaboration, the benefits of which have already been described in the previous chapter, can also pay dividends for well-established, medium-sized firms. Van Heyningen and Haward, for example, forged an alliance with the much larger and far more commercial practice Chapman Taylor to develop its competition entry for a £25 million building adjacent to the De La Warr Pavilion in Bexhill-on-Sea (see Figure 4.4). Although the scheme design belongs to VHH, the practice felt it needed to tap into Chapman Taylor's experience of handling large, administratively complex and politically sensitive projects to stand any chance of getting its entry short-listed. 'Whether we could have got on to the list without Chapman Taylor, I don't know. This is a very big job. We thought we wouldn't be considered if we didn't work with someone with that sort of experience,' says Joanna van Heyningen, who set up the practice in 1977 and was joined by husband Birkin Haward 5 years later.

VHH is also a member of the consortium PFI5, a band of five like-minded practices which have clubbed together to increase their chances of securing school work under PFI contracts. The practices – VHH, Feilden Clegg Bradley, Allford Hall Monaghan Morris, Hawkins\Brown and Penoyre & Prasad, along with project managers Buro Four – all have a fine track record in designing contemporary schools on an individual basis. But PFI5 will allow them to bid for 'bundles' of schools. The group has its own bank account and has standardized its fees as well as details like classroom sizes. 'We've come together

Figure 4.4 Van Heyningen and Haward collaborated with the much larger firm Chapman Taylor for this £25 million competition entry in Bexhill-on-Sea.

because this is the way schools are being procured nowadays. It makes it easy for a contractor to take us on,' says van Heyningen.

The group wasn't a random selection – the partners of these practices have known each other for years and have long benchmarked themselves against each other by comparing trade secrets such as fee scales, salaries and the number of pitches versus jobs won. So trust, which lies at the heart of the agreement, is well established. If they win a contract for five schools, they'll take one each. If there are only three schools, the practices with the most slack will get the work; and if the contract is especially large, Feilden Clegg Bradley (the biggest of the group with more than 100 staff) has the capacity to take on more than just a single project.

One of the reasons for this collaboration, says van Heyningen, is that these practices do not want to expand to get the work. Although a certain amount of growth and shrinkage is inevitable, some firms have an optimum size – beyond which they lose the culture, informality and cohesiveness which made them successful in the first place. For VHH, this number is around 25. 'We don't want our offices to be skewed by education work. If you took all the work yourself you would end up taking on staff to do it, and the practice would become a size it isn't supposed to be,' says van Heyningen, who adds that she doesn't want the practice to grow beyond 30 people.

CASE STUDY – Lifschutz Davidson

Alex Lifschutz believes the balance between size and informality, creativity and capability, lies at around 60 people. This size is just about small enough for everybody to know what's going on, he says, but big enough to handle really large jobs.

By early 2003 (when founding partner Ian Davidson died), the practice employed around 28 people, a figure which had grown to 45 by mid-2004. To effect a smooth transition to bigger numbers, Lifschutz and co-director Paul Sandilands installed a new corporate structure designed to ease their management responsibilities by sharing them out, and provide a clearer career path for junior staff.

This limited company is still led by Lifschutz and Sandilands, who joined the practice in 1988, but there are now four associate directors and three project directors to back them up. 'When you're 20-odd people, you can walk around with all the resourcing in your head. But a year ago we realized there was room at the top of our business,' says Sandilands, who adds that both he and Lifschutz were keen to promote internally. 'It's always been difficult to employ senior architects from outside the business. We've tried it and it's never quite worked out.'

The role of associate director represents a new strata of management, lying between Lifschutz/Sandilands and the three project directors. This is not a role that entails taking an equity share in the business (that is owned by just Lifschutz and Sandilands). Importantly, each of the four associate directors have shouldered some very specific responsibilities, quite apart from their day-to-day architectural duties:

- the office environment, including IT
- internal financial management, fees, salaries and time/money equations

- human resources, including training and appraisal, and
- new business, competitions, corporate identity and design standards.

Lifschutz is anxious, though, that the advent of these roles does not absolve everyone else from taking an interest in these subjects. Lifschutz is trying to create a practice along the lines of what he calls a 'European' management model, one which depends upon flexible staff with a mix of specialist and transferable skills. The opposite approach is the 'American' model, characterized by strict demarcation, functional separation and specialist managers.

He is adamant that he doesn't want the practice to grow as a series of 'firms within firms' where individual directors build their own teams. Instead, he envisages that the new directors will act as the centres of overlapping spheres of influence. This approach will, he hopes, provide a 'nucleus' around which different combinations of people can coalesce, as and when they're needed. In spite of strengthening the business hierarchy, the hope remains that the informality that has become a characteristic of the office will remain.

CASE STUDY – Ruddle Wilkinson

At the beginning of 1990 Peterborough-based practice Ruddle Wilkinson employed 60 people. By the end of the year, there were just 17. By the turn of the millennium, numbers had risen to 40, and there were more than 100 employees 4 years later. In fact, practice managers are fully prepared for staffing levels to reach 150 over coming years.

Importantly, this does not represent growth for growth's sake. The directors of this limited company have strong ideas about where they are going and what they need to do to get there. Indeed, the beginnings of a corporate vision predate the economic catastrophe that decimated the practice in the early 1990s.

Ruddle Wilkinson was founded in 1886 and is one of very few architectural practices that can trace its roots back that far.

A century later, a group of young partners began to realize that the practice had become, in a corporate sense, unfit and flabby. 'We felt strongly that the business had no strategy and no vision. It was just jogging along from one week to the next,' says John Durance, now chairman of the practice.

At the time, Ruddle Wilkinson was a strong regional firm, with outpost offices in towns like Spalding and Wisbech to take on small, low-budget jobs. It undertook a wide range of work – too wide, in fact. BT, the Regional Health Authority, small local businesses and individual home-owners all appeared on the client list. Durance estimated that 80 per cent of Ruddle Wilkinson's projects generated just 20 per cent of the practice's profit. Many projects even made a loss. The practice was also top heavy. One in seven of the staff was a partner.

In 1987, Durance and three other like-minded partners embarked on a programme of strategic planning – representing the first time in a generation that practice chiefs actually sat down to consider the long-term health and direction of the business. Significantly, older partners took a back seat and let them get on with it. In fact, three retired.

The four took a series of brave decisions. They closed most of the local offices and decided to turn down any work worth less than £250 000. They also decided to pitch themselves at the national market, for which they needed a stronger identity and focused marketing. Architectural marketing consultants Deborah Strattan and Amanda Reekie, now well-established, but then new and relatively untried, got the job.

Strattan and Reekie interviewed the practice's clients and drew up an objective list of strengths and weaknesses. The results were revealing. Generally, it was felt that, while Ruddle Wilkinson was competent and technically able, clients were not excited by the quality of the practice's design work. Effectively, Ruddle Wilkinson was trustworthy and would bring projects to a close on time and on budget, but few people felt the practice had the flair for design that would bring it success on the national stage. The practice was not 'design hungry', admits Durance.

The national market appealed to Durance because he suspected that bigger, blue chip clients would not only have bigger budgets, but that they represented less risk, would pay more promptly and that building programmes would be carefully scheduled – enabling the practice to plan ahead more effectively. 'I sit here 15 years later and that has turned out to be absolutely the case', he says.

In a sense, the recession of the early 1990s did Ruddle Wilkinson a favour. By forcing the practice to lay off most of its staff, the partners could change the profile of the workforce when conditions improved and expansion became a possibility. Durance is now confident that the balance between competent/trustworthy/reliable and conceptual/imaginative has now been struck. The British Airport Authority seems to think so, which signed Ruddle Wilkinson up to a 5-year framework agreement late in 2003 (along with Foster, Grimshaw, Reid Architecture and the Parr Partnership).

In 1991, the practice incorporated as a limited company, relieving the partners of the burden of risking their personal assets by making them directors. Also, says Durance, the move forced senior staff to focus more on financial performance: 'Until then, we had no proper concept of profit.' The practice now has five directors, each with their own specific area of responsibility:

- Management strategy and human resources (undertaken by Durance)
- Marketing and business development
- Technology and quality assurance
- Finance
- Running the London office (a position filled by Clare Devine – a senior, external appointment which is rare at the practice. Poached from London-based Shepard Epstein Hunter, Devine had experience that others at Ruddle Wilkinson lacked).

But the hard-nosed Durance had a further trick up his sleeve. As chairman of his local Training and Enterprise Council throughout the 1990s, Durance had become a champion of the human resources mantra that 'people are a company's most valuable asset'. Consequently, he introduced the concept of formal training to the practice, on top of standard CPD. As well as laying on technical programmes in subjects like computing (a black art in architecture until very recently), Durance insisted that staff enrol on short, sharp courses in subjects like time management, team working and basic supervision.

The overall idea was three-fold: training can be perceived as a reward in itself, contributing to staff feelings of inclusivity and advancement. It filled the gaps in standard architectural education and allowed all staff, architectural and otherwise, to develop to company-wide standards. And training in the 'soft' people-centred subjects began to create a closer match between the practice and its target clients. Furthermore, Durance kick-started a profit-sharing scheme and began to instil a sense of 'open management' culture throughout the office. Now, every employee is broadly familiar with trading conditions and business performance, and each has a personal training and development plan which is closely linked to the strategic goals of the practice. This last point is important, and is a requirement of the government-sponsored Investor in People programme, conceived to recognize sound management practice. Ruddle Wilkinson was only the fifth practice in the UK to qualify for IIP status, when awarded its plaque in 1996.

Overall, Durance has done something right. Apart from signing a deal with BAA, the practice has worked out similar agreements with Tube Lines (the private sector body tackling the rejuvenation of the capital's underground infrastructure), the Royal Bank of Scotland, Marks & Spencer and Ikea. Now, a staggering 75 per cent of the practice's work is generated in this way. The scene is now set for further expansion, perhaps to 150 staff, which would represent something like a 50 per cent increase from the size of the practice when this book went to press. Durance would also like to increase efficiency so that a greater proportion of turnover becomes profit – the figure is currently around 7.5 per cent, which isn't bad but would be more respectable in the teens.

Durance offers the following action points for practices considering expansion:

• Work hard to form a board of directors that shares a common vision and speaks with a single voice.

- Listen to people from outside the profession, perhaps formalized as non-executives, to help form a business strategy.
- Once you have settled on your goals, understand that you might have to be flexible about when you achieve them.
- Be prepared to take risks, and understand how to manage them.
- Embark on change in the following manner: plan – do – evaluate – replan.
- Benchmark yourself against competitors, even if it means sharing information.
- Match recruitment and selection procedures with company aims.
- Communicate with staff, so they know exactly where they stand and where the company is going.

CHAPTER FIVE

Managing the office

It has long been a cliché among management thinkers that staff – occasionally (frighteningly) called 'human capital' – are the most valuable asset of any business. That is true if you have the right staff. A piece of advice often whispered by architects, but rarely employed, is this: don't employ an architect if you only need a technician. Employing architects merely through force of habit can lead to frustrated employees and needlessly inflated wage bills.

Robert Adam Architects, with an international reputation for classical-style buildings, employs more technicians than archi-tects. Sixty strong, Robert Adam employs around 15 architects, or people who are working towards their Part 3, and twice as many technicians. Even one of the practice's four directors didn't train as an architect (he is a technician with a degree in building). This is a practice with 90–100 projects on the go at any one time, ranging from one-off houses to masterplanning, with values of between £250 000 and £20 million.

Taking on staff is a major undertaking, and many architects prefer to stay small simply to absolve themselves from the responsibility of it. Chapter 1 mentions the benefits of engaging people as consultants, which both simplifies and reduces the tax overhead. This is a pefectly legitimate and acceptable way of working, not least because the culture of networking and collaboration is almost second nature to people in the architecture profession. Although consultants need not show any particular loyalty to a practice, this style of employment does allow a business to test someone out before offering them a full-time position.

Consultants are particularly useful to help practices cope with sudden workload bulges, and recruitment agencies are only too happy to supply them. Be warned, though, that charges for agency staff can cost around 15 per cent more than staff you find yourself. Architects also complain that recruitment agencies put their own interests first – one complaint is that, having helped you find a full-time staff member, there is nothing to stop an agency staying in touch with the new recruit and keeping them informed of new opportunities (the agency takes a fee with each appointment).

Robert Adam, who says that adverts in the trade press don't attract the right sort of people in the right sort of numbers, has taken on a part-time recruitment consultant to help explore alternative recruitment methods. One tactic has been to launch an annual travelling scholarship worth £1500 to help a young architect study classical architecture and traditional urbanism. Another tactic is to try to establish informal networks among like-minded architects. Recruitment is a serious issue for the practice, even though staff turnover is extremely low. People stay for an average of 5 years but, with 60 staff, that means one person leaves roughly every month. London-based RHWL has also launched its own recruitment initiative. From September 2004, the practice will take on six Part 1 students for 1 year, after which they could be eligible for Part 2 sponsorship and a job offer.

Employing staff also brings with it a mountain of legal responsibilities. It is not the purpose of this book to explain the detail of employment legislation, which is better explained in other specialist publications (bodies such as the Chartered Institute of Personnel and Development, and the excellent website www. compactlaw.co.uk can also help). But, briefly, all employers need to abide by legislation governing equal opportunities, working hours and employment protection. It may come as a surprise to some practices, which pay late-working staff in pizzas rather than hard cash, that the Working Time Regulations place a ceiling of 48 hours on the working week, unless an employee declares in writing that they wish to work beyond this limit.

The fact is that the architectural community is so small and interlinked that people rarely resort to the law to remedy what they see as poor employment practice. Women, who represent only around 13 per cent of architects in spite of the fact that they make up one third of architecture students, quietly leave the profession rather than press for improved flexible working packages. But it is worth remembering that the Employment Rights Act (1996) opens employers up to heavy financial penalties if they are found, by employment tribunals, to be in breach of the law. Unfair dismissal, for example, can cost an employer £55 000.

The simplest way to deal with the law is to be fair and transparent in all employment-related matters. Recruitment decisions should be seen to have been taken against clear and objective criteria; and the same applies to cases of dismissal or redundancy (last in, first out is seen as a legitimate policy). Put everything in writing. Provide employees with an unambiguous contract of employment which includes the following: rates of pay, working hours, holiday entitlement, disciplinary procedures and a job description. Importantly, seriously entertain the idea of introducing flexible working practices if an employee makes a request. Flexible working can provide enormous benefits, especially if arrangements can help retain someone of talent. Refusing to even consider an employee's request is dangerous; if an employer is found to have willfully made an employee's life so difficult that they invite a resignation, that counts as constructive dismissal, which is illegal. Flexible working tends to benefit female staff, and some practices have tried hard to attract women architects by drawing up imaginative employment regimes. RHWL, for example, operates a policy which allows mothers to design their working day around the hours of their child's creche. Southwark's Building Design Service adheres to general council policy by offering flexitime, which allows staff to fit a 36-hour week around a 'core' working day of 10 to 4.

Beyond the legal contract, it is not uncommon to hear members of the personnel profession speak of the 'psychological contract' – a sort of unspoken agreement about the expectations of employer and employee. The traditional psychological contract caused employees to believe that their jobs would last a lifetime. In place of this, people have developed more subtle expectations – hopes of stimulation, satisfaction, a creative environment, early responsibility, career advancement and so on. These are messages that employers can communicate both intentionally and accidentally. Either way, this is a very real phenomenon, and any mismatch between expectations and reality can cause resentment, low morale and high staff turnover.

The Industrial Society, now rebranded as the Work Foundation, once ran a course in basic supervisory skills. A standard feature of the course was the following (true) anecdote. A large company commissioned a piece of research in order to discover the motivations of its staff for bothering to come to work. Generally, everybody thought that people above and below them in the corporate hierarchy was motivated by money, although everyone individually was motivated by factors such as job satisfaction, flexible working and development opportunities. This is not to suggest that salaries are unimportant (they are, and practices should try to benchmark themselves against their peers), but it shows that employers must consider the 'softer' and less obvious tactics that combine to create an efficient and loyal workforce. A succession policy is important for two reasons: it shows staff that there may be room for promotion and ensures the continual survival of the business. Training can also be viewed as a reward for good performance. Promotion, matched by just a modest pay rise, is also a useful personnel tool. The term 'associate' is over-used, but is meaningful if it formalizes a genuine set of responsibilities.

Large practices, such as HOK and Nicholas Grimshaw employ their own full-time personnel specialists, but this will be beyond the means of small- and medium-sized firms. Any practice beyond the size of three or four people will benefit from employing a part-time practice manager, even for just one day a week. Larger firms, of around a dozen people, would do well to consider employing someone full-time. A good practice manager will make a tremendous difference to the efficiency of a business by bringing a coherent methodology to administration, freeing up designers to concentrate on what they were trained to do. A practice manager is not a PA or a secretary; instead, a PM's duties include book-keeping, cash flow and timesheet management, and perhaps a little human resources and public relations. Vick Bain, a freelance practice manager since 1998 and director of The Creative Support Agency, says her clients (which include Tony Fretton, Sarah Featherstone and MUF) permit her a big voice. She tells them what they're allowed to spend, how much they need to bill and will point out if she thinks a client is pitching its fees too low.

'I'll say "Look, these are your minimum outgoings, so you've got to raise, say, £25 000-worth of invoices this month",' says Bain. 'All practices have the same issues, they're just bigger or smaller in scale.'

Bain adds that a good practice manager needs to understand the particular pressures, and chaos, of the creative industries. They must also want to do the job and not drift into it by accident or harbour their own ambitions to be a designer. 'A good practice manager must be doing it because they really want to,' she says.

Any practice will eventually have to face up to the issue of succession – filling the shoes of the founding partner after they retire. Very small practices need not trouble themselves with succession, because the founder and the business might be one and the same. Alternatively, a sole practitioner with a valuable client list might have something valuable to sell before winding the practice up. In most cases, though, succession is important. Effective succession plans smooth the path from one generation to another and act as a psychological comforter for employees. Staff working for ageing partners who have made no noises about their successors will feel nothing if not vulnerable.

Succession is best planned well in advance, and it needs to be conducted with the utmost care. Successors stand the best chance of carrying the business forward if they have emerged from within the practice, which means that senior external appointees need to be brought in some years before they are needed to take the helm. Tim Hamilton, of Chelsea-based Hamilton Associates, recruited Robin Partington from Foster and Partners in 2002 as part of a long-term plan to beef up his senior team before easing himself into retirement.

'In our profession people are very secretive. They build up businesses which are highly personal, but then they don't want to face the inevitable and let go,' says Hamilton. 'I was smart enough to see it coming in time for succession to become a natural process rather than an arbitrary one. There will be no jockeying for position; the whole aim has been to avoid internal politics.'

Some architects are not just happy to let go – they are also prepared to see their names erased from the headed paper. George Ferguson, a founding partner of Bristol-based Acanthus Ferguson Mann, is now just one of six practice directors (and owns just one sixth of the firm). Directors are aged between 37 and 57, and Ferguson is confident that the practice employs the right people to take the business forward without him. Eventually, he says, the practice will probably be called Acanthus FM. As explained elsewhere in this chapter, Robert Adam is thinking along much the same lines.

RHWL provides a decent example of solid succession planning. Renton Associates was formed when Andrew Renton broke from Basil Spence in 1960, becoming RHWL 2 years later when partnerships were offered to Peter Howard, Humphrey Wood and Gerrald Levine.

Figure 5.1 Controversial tower proposal from RHWL, for a site near Waterloo station, London.

In the early days the practice had the spirit of a gentleman's club, a 'smallish, rather intellectual' outfit, recalls Geoff Mann, who joined the practice in 1970 and was promoted to partner 9 years later. By that time the practice had grown to 130 staff, and it continued to expand until its peak in the mid-1980s when the staff roll call topped 200. Numbers have since dropped back to around 150, but what is interesting about this practice is that fundamental management principles have remained unchanged throughout the ebb and flow of its life.

Renton has since died, while H, W and L have all since retired, leaving the practice in the hands of six partners. Interestingly, none of the directors have an equity stake in the practice – all benefit from an equal share of the profits instead of a regular salary, and partnerships do not come with a price. 'It makes us genuine pals and there's nothing corrosive in the business,' says Mann.

Apart from Nick Thompson and Barry Pritchard, who jointly run the Arts Team, the partners each run their own multidisciplinary teams and are backed up by salaried junior partners and associates. Importantly, full-blown partners are not drawn from this heirarchy for reasons of seniority or long-service, which often makes decisions 'quite tricky', admits Mann. Promotions to the top table remain unplanned – the idea is not one of filling vacancies, but of securing people who have proved their worth.

'We've survived the third generation and now we're planning the fourth, but we're allowing that new generation to happen naturally. We're looking for younger people in the practice who will maintain this seamless progression from one generation to another,' says Mann.

☞ **Action points**

- Don't employ an architect if you need a technician.
- Actively consider opportunities for flexible working.
- Draw up an equal opportunities statement – even if it is simple: '[practice name] is an equal opportunities employer'.
- Draw up an unambiguous contract of employment (see Appendix E).
- Draw up job descriptions, possibly including personal objectives, against which people can be assessed if you decide to put in place a staff appraisal process.
- Try to be fair and transparent in all employment matters, especially in disciplinary cases and when making people redundant. Put important decisions in writing and explain your reasoning against clear criteria.
- Understand the 'psychological contract' between staff and your practice.
- Develop a succession policy, either by recruiting outsiders or coaching junior staff.
- Employ a practice manager, on a part-time basis for small practices.

- Consider engaging people as consultants before taking them on as staff. This provides an opportunity for them to prove themselves.

CASE STUDY – Robert Adam Architects

Robert Adam takes a dim view of the excessive hours often demanded by architectural employers. As mentioned in Chapter 1, staff at Winchester-based Robert Adam Architects receive overtime payments, which are charged back to the client. Adam believes that, if a practice has a good idea of how long a job will take, there is no need to make demands on people's personal lives. Regularly demanding overtime from staff is, he says, 'immoral and managerially unsatisfying'. Also, if architects fail to take all-night working into account it is impossible to arrive at a proper understanding of the cost of a job.

'I would consider that we'd be seriously mismanaging our firm if we always insisted on people doing overtime,' says Adam.

In one respect Adam can make striking statements like these because he is fortunate enough to work for wealthy clients who will pay what he believes he is worth. On the other hand, Adam has invested heavily in administration systems which keep projects, time management and billing firmly on track. Of the practice's 60 staff, 10 fill administrative roles. Indeed, accounting is handled by no less than four different people – practice manager Nigel Afford (who doubles up as secretary to the board), an accounts manager, a book-keeper and an external accountant who is mainly used for auditing. Afford says his responsibilities for recording working hours against jobs (using Orica Software's Timemaster program) and invoicing clients is 'critical' to the success of the practice.

At the top of the practice there are four (equity-holding) directors, providing a ratio of one director for 11 architectural staff. Traditionally, the ratio hovers around 10 or 12:1, a balance which Adam wants to retain. A fifth director, holding no equity at first, is likely to be appointed, which will also help Adam deal with succession issues.

Adam takes succession seriously, and the 56-year-old wants the practice to continue after his retirement (when a director reaches 60, he has to ask the board's permission to remain, which Adam is likely to do). In fact, Adam was recruited as part of a succession planning initiative of a former generation. The practice has its origins in the 1950s when it was set up as Evans Roberts and Partners, which Adam describes as a 'pretty standard, provincial practice' with no particular aesthetic preference. Adam joined in 1977 as part of an effort to recruit young, senior staff. His classical style became the most recognizable brand during the 1980s and Adam rebadged the firm in 1992, since when it has become the largest classical firm in Europe.

Adam is now prepared to consider a future for the practice without him. Once he retires, he has no problem with the business dropping his name and finding a new one – in fact, he fully expects this to happen. The same degree of humility applies to his selection of directors. Directors, says Adam, should not be mere ciphers; instead, directors should be challenging, confident agents of change. 'If you bring in a director who doesn't make an impact on the firm, then they're not worth having as a director. This is a very important principle; they've got to change things,' says Adam.

CASE STUDY – MUF

Now 10 years old, MUF's survival is remarkable – after just 3 years in practice the firm landed a £5 million contract to design the Local Zone for the Millennium Dome, but then lost it because of 'insubordination' to the client. This meant that after tasting, briefly, the fruits of success (generous fees, being paid on time, hopping in and out of taxis) the practice had to regroup and start all over again – and pay off a £25 000 loan. Since then, MUF has remained just as self-confident and determined to plough its own furrow. Staff at this eight-strong firm do not work weekends, benefit from almost unheard-of flexibility in the way they order their working lives, and turn down work they find less than interesting.

Partner Liza Fior says the decision to cut weekend work has barely made a difference to the performance of the practice, while motherhood probably means less informal networking and 'schmoozing'. And the interest threshold which potential jobs must reach before they become tempting is linked to a deeply-held belief that there is nothing wrong with small, barely profitable projects as long as they are professionally challenging: 'If you don't pay yourself a huge amount of money then it has to be interesting; otherwise, you might as well be on a supermarket management training scheme,' says Fior.

The key to MUF's survival is very probably its approach to staffing. Of the eight staff, there are three mothers and just one

Figure 5.2   The Hypocaust building is probably this small practice's major achievement to date.

Figure 5.3   MUF's £800, 000 Hypocaust building for St Albans, won by competition in 1999.

male. Part-time, flexible working, with the chance to take prolonged sabbaticals, is part of the culture of the office. One member of staff works just 3 days a week in order to study for a law degree. The two partners have awarded themselves 6 months' paid maternity leave, which is a perk they are considering extending to long-serving staff. Consequently, staff retention is high, which saves on the cost and uncertainty of recruitment, and is a reassuring measure of stability for clients (especially when projects spend a long time in gestation, like the £800 000 Hypocaust building in St Albans, completed in 2004 but won in 1999) (see Figures 5.2 and 5.3).

Enlightened personnel policies go hand-in-hand with strict business administration procedures. Since appointing Vick Bain as a part-time practice manager (who works 1 day a week), the practice has become better at managing time-sheets and working out the relative profitablity of different jobs. MUF has also developed an electronic cash-flow management system and become far more ruthless about chasing invoices, a job which is handled by Bain. 'It's great not to have to ring clients yourself, asking for money. You have to try and keep a distance,' says Fior.

CHAPTER SIX

IT

Apart from the cost of staff, IT could easily be a practice's biggest business investment, and should take up at least 1 per cent of annual turnover. A figure of 3 per cent would, however, be nearer the mark. Architects need to understand that IT should be an on-going concern rather than a one-off burden which has to be shouldered once every few years. The cost of hardware, software, updates, security, trouble-shooting and archiving can be considerable, and no business should underestimate the importance of maintaining a reliable computing infrastructure. In many ways, just like staff, IT *is* the business.

Purchasing decisions are often difficult, protracted affairs and wise practices will seek the advice of consultants before making big investments. Such is the pace of change that only very few architects manage to keep abreast of developments in both the architectural and IT arenas. Broadly, though, it is a fact of life that software is often more expensive than hardware, and practices must decide which programs they want to use before making computer choices. Occasionally, this is a decision that is made for you; some large clients have software preferences, and it is useful to use the same design packages as your consultants. Crucially, software choices can dictate whether practices opt for PCs or Macs, or a mixture of the two.

In spite of its powerful reinvention in recent years, architects' practices appear to be slowly abandoning the Mac because the two most influential software houses – Bentley, which produces Microstation, and Autodesk, developer of Autocad – write software exclusively for PCs. Although a useful piece of software called VirtualPC can make a Mac behave like a PC, this is not an ideal solution. If you are stuck on using either Microstation or Autocad, then investing in PCs is probably the wisest choice.

However, if you are ambivalent (or wedded to Apple) there is a wide range of software choices. In terms of design packages, ArchiCAD, Vectorworks, Form Z and the excellent newcomer SketchUp work on either platform. Also, before making a purchase, think hard about what you want your software to do, because there are perfectly good alternatives for the budget conscious. For example, Bentley's Powerdraft is effectively a slimmed down version of Microstation for a quarter of the price. Similarly, Autocad LT provides a good alternative to the full version. Finally, even if PCs look like a sensible choice, it might be worth having at least one Mac in the office to take advantage of the amount of free software these machines come with – iMovie and iPhoto, for example, are first-class presentation and sound-editing tools. Apart from that, Macs are less likely to be the target of viruses.

IT is a much misunderstood thing. Too often architects feel powerless in the face of a necessary evil but, in fact, there is a lot that practices can do to make themselves the master of their computing investment. In any practice there is often one member of staff who is more technologically savvy than the rest, and there is nothing wrong with utilizing these skills and even formalizing them into a job description. Equally, it makes good sense to sign a contract with a specialist IT consultancy, as there is a limit to what the office enthusiast is capable of (or even willing to tackle, given other job commitments). There is an almost endless supply of computer consultants for hire, including a small number of excellent specialists who originally trained as architects. It is worthwhile paying one a monthly retainer to have them at your beck and call. A good consultant will not only be able to advise on hard/software selection, but will be able to customize it, trouble-shoot, optimize your network, keep your virus protection systems up-to-date and keep hackers out. It's worth pointing out that the reputation of Foster and Partners is not just the result of design talent – the practice has also been working closely with Bentley's head of development, Robert Aish, to increase the capability of Microstation and make it work harder than the off-the-shelf product. KPF has been doing the same thing.

Apart from design, well-run architecture practices will be using IT as the backbone of their administration systems. Some off-the-peg systems have already been mentioned (see Chapter 3) but there are others: Planchest is now well-established as an archiving, project management and scheduling tool, for example, while PH-Media's TIMEminder (used by McAslan and Partners, Hawkins\Brown and Stephenson Bell) is a handy tool for matching working hours, costs and invoices. This piece of software is doubly useful because it provides a database against which all a practice's jobs can be measured; and by monitoring the profitability of jobs (by sector, size and team) a practice can make informed decisions about the future direction of its work.

Practices which really want to harness the power of IT to integrate their business, and therefore use computing as a strategic business tool, will probably have to develop their own system. Sheppard Robson, for example, has invested considerable effort developing what it calls a 'data hub', served by a pair of powerful Microsoft SQL client server databases that allow staff to cross-reference the metadata of hundreds of thousands of files in an almost unimaginable number of ways. Projects, images, details of staff and subcontractors, and a myriad of other resources are available to allow architects to, for example, put together bids and tenders with relative ease. The resource will also include 250 of Sheppard Robson's most frequently used details and building models, so that anything from a lift core to a fire strategy can be quickly summoned up. This has the advantage of both saving time and anchoring expertise firmly into the corporate memory. Half a million records (including 3000 projects, 10 000 contacts and nearly 170 000 drawings and revisions) are securely protected.

Most impressive of all is that the user is largely unaware of the different software packages that that have been bolted on to the hub in order to make any sense of the data inside – Exchange 2000, the company intranet, the Snowdrop HR system, Union Square financial reporting packages, Word, a customized version of PlanChest and (lastly) Microstation all feed into, and off, the hub. Importantly, these programs remain all but invisible, and the user can, for example, summon up project images, slot them into a document template and email them to subcontractors without self-consciously moving from one program to another.

More visibly, IT provides the tool by which architects generally display their work. Slick, photorealistic images are now relatively simple to create (thanks to developments in the movie industry) and have become so commonplace as to be almost boring. Sophisticated imaging is now something that all practices have to take seriously, whether it's undertaken in-house or by an external consultant. Often clients demand it, either as part of an effort to win planning consent or to use in a marketing campaign. Consequently, many architects find that they are being pushed into drawing up highly resolved schemes long before they are good and ready. Indeed, it is not uncommon for visualization specialists to work on the detailing, while the rest of the design team are finalizing massing studies.

Some clients are proving so demanding that they even expect practices to collude in the marketing effort to a far greater extent than many architects expect. Images of bright new developments have to be filled with the sort of bright young people these buildings are aimed at – people who wear the right clothes, sip the right drinks and drive the right cars. Occasionally, the model is pulled apart to allow a camera to record a view that would, in real life, be impossible. This kind of work takes time, and it is unlikely that smaller practices will be able to afford to take it on in-house. Often, even very large practices outsource particularly demanding images – Alsop regularly uses Tekuchi, for example, and RHWL commissioned GMJ to produce a single, seductive image of a tower proposal for London's Waterloo (see Figure 5.1). There is a way of staying small and benefiting from expensive visualization services – hire a specialist to work for you, and offer their services on the open market in lean periods. Van Heyningen and Haward does this, through its off-shoot MGi.

The problem with outsourcing is that the visualization and design processes are carried out in isolation from one another. The most productive use of advanced rendering techniques is when convincing images can be produced in parallel with design development, as a way of testing and interrogating the design programme. Such exactitude might even be kept hidden from clients who prefer a soft-focus, water-coloured rendition of their investment, in which case, a program like Piranesi can prove invaluable.

The future of visualization is almost certainly allied to the design process, probably as a result of 3D modelling and rapid rendering which will allow designers to take a look around their virtual buildings at every single stage of the design process. If programs like Cadai and RTRE become widespread, creating a bridge between architectural design and computer gaming, architects could get instant, realistic, 3D feedback as soon as they make a mark. In fact, considering that a good deal of the software used by architects originated in the movie and computer games industries, it is a wonder that 'real-time' design is taking so long to catch on.

Real-time (what University of Westminster professor Murray Fraser calls 'fully-immersive, navigable environments') is a challenging prospect. Not only might presentation pieces be generated all the way through the design process, but clients could be able to steer their own way around virtual buildings without being restricted by the predetermined paths of video fly-throughs. Give the scheme a narrative, and you've got a game on your hands.

☞ **Action points**

- Spend at least 1 per cent of your annual turnover on IT.
- If you are not large enough to employ a full-time IT manager, find an IT consultant to help you source, install and maintain your systems. Look for someone who has experience with other architectural clients.
- Be aware that IT covers more than design programs and email. Well-run offices use dedicated software packages covering finance, time-management and data storage/archiving.
- Help-desks can be expensive and frustrating. Join web-based forums and chat-rooms, where users frequently exchange advice and trouble-shooting tips.
- Remember that software is open to being customized. Talk to the software vendor/consultants about tweaking the code to make a program more suitable to your needs.
- Match your imagery to your client. Some clients want photo-realistic visuals – others still prefer watercolour.
- Record serial numbers, version numbers, upgrades, and purchase dates for all software. Keep this information safe and copy this to your insurers.
- Make a duplicate copy of all software. Keep it in the office and securely store the original, preferably off site.
- Register your software, the junk marketing mail is a small price to pay for proving your ownership if software is lost.
- When replacing stolen computers, increase security to deter repeat burglaries (thieves will return more than once). Visit www.top-tec.co.uk for a range of security enclosures and www.kensington.com for systems suitable for iMacs and lap-tops. Don't leave new computer boxes in the street for collection, break them up into bin bags before putting them out for the binmen.

CASE STUDY – Broadway Malyan

In 2004 Broadway Malyan, one of the UK's largest practices, introduced a highly-automated intranet system to help the practice manage the 700 projects it has on the go at any one time. Developed over a 3-year period, the business process system has been designed to increase efficiency, improve communications and provide a reliable audit-trail of who did what, when.

Each project has a home-page listing the job leader, job number, the client and other key information. The system announces each stage of a project and highlights which tasks need to be undertaken. As tasks are carried out, the system automatically ticks a completion box. 'It is an interactive system which focuses on ensuring that all relevant tasks are completed at exactly the right stage of a project. This system has been developed to do everything automatically,' says Adrian Burton, senior architect and business process facilitator at the practice.

If a team member opens a document, makes a change and saves it, the system records who did it, when, and indicates the next stage. A project review reminder automatically appears on the team's screens every 3 months. Once a meeting date has passed, the system prompts the user to complete a project review form. It also records project completion dates – 11 months later, a message appears on the job leader's monitor to prompt them to contact the client to make sure the building is living up to its promise.

CASE STUDY – Jonathan Reeves Architecture (jra)

Jonathan Reeves is a Bristol-based sole practitioner whose business would have been unviable, even unthinkable, a decade ago. But this Mac enthusiast, complete with all the accoutrements of the modern computing age (broadband, iChat, email, a dual processor, 2Ghz Apple G5 and a G4 laptop) is able to punch far above the weight expected of a one-man practice.

Reeves graduated from Sheffield University in 1991 but, because of the economic situation of the time, could not find a practice to offer him year-out experience. So he stayed at college and took a masters degree in architecture and computing instead, after which he took his Part 3. With the economy in better health by 1995, and with the demand for computer-literate graduates on the increase, Reeves landed a string of jobs in London, and also a spell in Sydney practice Vim Design.

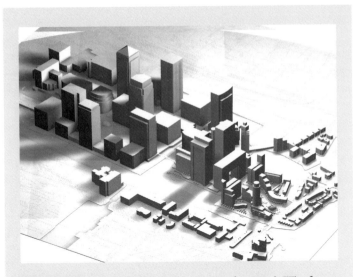

Figure 6.1 This masterplanning exercise for Wood Wharf, near London's Canary Wharf, is the result of collaboration between two sole practitioners.

Since setting up on his own in 2000 (helped at first by regular work with what was then Feilden Clegg) Reeves' practice has separated into three areas: collaborative design work, visualizing and CAD training. His website is the source of regular commissions, with a serious enquiry arriving roughly once a fortnight. He has now collaborated with Oxfordshire-based design firm BRED on a number of design jobs without even having had a face-to-face meeting. These commissions were not undertaken without some misgivings, however, and he was especially concerned about being paid by someone he had never met. Fortunately, BRED has turned out to pay more promptly than many other clients.

Word of mouth has also been an important source of work, notably his collaborative effort with Nick Kuhn-Architect, a Bath-based, ex-BDP partner specializing in masterplanning. Using CAD design software as 'digital clay', the pair successfully masterplanned the new Wood Wharf commercial and residential district (adjacent to London's Canary Wharf) for British Waterways. Their scheme, which went through 30–40 different versions, was adopted in December 2003 (see Figure 6.1).

For a sole practitioner, Reeves' client list is impressive, including: Hampshire County Council (where he undertakes training), Acanthus Ferguson Mann and the Building Research Establishment, where he is collaborating on a new generation of secondary school. The advent of email and being able to quickly swap CAD and PDF files lies at the heart of his business model, which is predicated on the fact that IT allows him to work remotely, efficiently and often without the need to travel.

Design work is often the result of physical proximity and personal contact, but Reeves' experience shows that, with a good brief, face-to-face contact is not necessarily a requirement for a successful outcome. When personal meetings become essential, though, there is always the laptop, which was employed to good effect in Nick Kuhn's office. 'We couldn't have done what we did without the technology, or by using the software in the way that we did. But through the process of doing it we struck up a very close personal relationship,' says Reeves.

Reeves uses:
- Vectorworks 11 and SketchUP, for design, layout and 3D modelling
- Art.Lantis 4.5 and Cinema 4D R8 for visualizing and animation
- Photoshop CS for image editing
- InDesign CS for brochure design, and
- GoLive CS for website design.

Debt
collection

Debtor collection performance standard: 14-day settlement terms

Drawn up by Sobell Rhodes Chartered Accountants

Stages

1. Invoice is raised for payment (day 0)
2. One week after invoice, statement is sent (day 7)
3. Two weeks after invoice, due date for payment (day 14)
4. Within 1 week of the due date, a phone call and important reminder notice to be sent, together with a copy of the invoice (day 21)
5. One week later, a further phone call followed by written confirmation by fax in the normal style of a letter (day 28)
6. One week later, overdue account notice to be sent, together with a statement (day 35)
7. One week later, final reminder notice (day 42)
8. Action notice. This to be sent by fax, by post or, if appropriate, by courier.

Debtor collection performance standard: 30-day settlement terms

Stages

1. Invoice is raised for payment (day 0)
2. Three weeks after invoice, statement is sent (day 21)
3. 30 days after invoice, due date for payment (day 30)
4. Within 1 week of the due date, a phone call and important reminder notice to be sent, together with a copy of the invoice (day 37)
5. One week later, a further phone call followed by written confirmation by fax in the normal style of a letter (day 44)
6. One week later, overdue account notice to be sent, together with a statement (day 51)
7. One week later, final reminder notice (day 58)
8. Action notice. This to be sent by fax, by post or, if appropriate by courier.

Stage 2 – 1 week before due date, by post

Statement

Please note that your account will soon be due for payment and settlement by the due date shown below would be very much appreciated.

Amount due:
Due date for payment:

Stage 4 – within 1 week after due date, phone call plus by post

Important reminder

Please give this matter your urgent attention

I am sorry that you have missed the date by which your account was due.

If you have any queries or difficulties in settling the amount, please ring us.

Alternatively, please send your payment as a matter of priority.

Attached is a copy of the outstanding fee note.

If this notice has crossed in the post with your cheque, thank you.

Amount overdue:
Due date for payment:

Credit Manager

Stage 5 – 1 week after stage 4, phone call, followed up by written confirmation by fax

I refer to our telephone conversation this morning/afternoon and confirm. . .
. . . . .

Stage 6 – 1 week after phone call

Overdue account

Attached is a statement of your account which is now seriously overdue.

Please settle this amount immediately

Amount:
Days overdue:

In accordance with our terms of engagement, we reserve the right to charge interest on the account at the rate of 1.5 per cent for every month or part of a month that the account is outstanding beyond the 14 day credit limit.

Stage 7 – 1 week later

Final reminder

To date, your account has still not been settled despite our reminders.

We would advise you that until payment has been made, no further work will be carried out on your behalf, and interest will be charged from the date that the account was due.

Please give this matter your immediate attention.

Due date:
Amount outstanding:
Interest:
Total:

Stage 8 – final stage, by fax, post or courier (if costs allow)

Action

Set out below is a statement of your account with us which is still outstanding, together with the interest which has accrued as set out in our terms of engagement.

If you do not take action and settle this amount by return of post, application will be made through the courts to recover the debt.

Your prompt response to this reminder is essential in order to avoid you receiving a summons from the courts.

Amount outstanding:
Interest:
Total:

In-house PR office versus external consultant

Benefits of in-house PR

- In-house staff are close to the source. Having a press officer in place means news is generated at corporate/project level. Also, an in-house person will be able to gather material and process approvals at a much faster rate than an external consultant.
- Journalists like a good press officer. Having one point of contact for a firm, and the confidence that a request will be responded to quickly, is a huge asset. Journalists trust good press officers and, once a good relationship is established, will come back to them for help when researching features.
- If a firm is brimming with publishable activity, PR will be a full-time role anyway.

93

- Good relationships with busy staff are essential if a press officer is to get the information needed. This is harder to achieve as a consultant.
- An in-house PR officer can introduce a procedure instructing all staff to work through the press desk whenever approached by a journal. This will avoid any clash of press commitments to different journals on exclusives. It will also protect staff from inadvertently giving out information about embargoed projects or speaking off the record.
- Being around the office: a staff member will not be logging a time sheet, and will have the flexibility to travel between offices and sites to achieve information gathering and dissemination. They have their ear to the ground.
- In-house press officers are also frequently responsible for the firm's internal communications, staff newsletter, etc.
- Senior management time: a consultant will need more management time for meetings, briefings and approvals. A consultant can be reliant on the client identifying a story/project and asking for it to be taken forward; an in-house team member with a nose for news will just get on with it.

Benefits of consultant PR

- A practice's size/workload may not be sufficient to support a full-time staff member. Consultants can be brought in when necessary.
- Consultants can be used as much, or as little, as you like. It might be worthwhile paying a monthly retainer for heavy workloads, or engaging one on a daily basis for one-off projects.
- Consultants can do the creative thinking for you. Often practices, including in-house PR teams, are so busy with detail that it is difficult for them to step back and see a wider picture. Consultants should be able to offer fresh thinking.
- Consultants will probably have a good knowledge of matters which a practice will need only rarely – for example, event management, exhibitions and publishing. In-house staff will generally expect external help with this sort of work.

- Consultants will have an understanding of a wide range of businesses. Although they will be bound by client confidentiality, consultants will know what works (and what doesn't).
- Good consultants are respected by the press, and journalists will often call them for advice or to help them complete a story. A typical question might be: 'We're doing an article on housing – do you know anyone?'
- Consultants can be used as an independent sounding board and should offer impartial advice. They will remain unaffected by internal office politics/personal relations, which can be the downfall of an in-house press officer.
- Consultants can help practices set up their own in-house teams. They will often help recruit, train and coach in-house staff before leaving a client to go it alone.

Person specification for in-house PR

A graduate in communications, with one or two jobs behind them, looking for more responsibility. A person of this calibre should be well-rehearsed in all aspects of running a proactive press office, including writing business-to-business press releases, as well as technical feature articles. Unless recruited from within the built environment community, the person will need a fast track introduction to the construction industry and key press. Preferably a member of IPR or CIM.

. . . or . . .

An architectural/technical graduate looking to make a career move into press/business development. In this case, support in how to set up and run a press office will be needed, probably provided via a consultant.

Resources for in-house staff

- Mediadisk (or similar) on-line press listing licence: necessary to research journals and build accurate press lists. License fee

95

for one concurrent user for all media Europe-wide is around £6000 a year. A UK-only press list is a lot cheaper.

- Mobile phone
- Small budget for hospitality
- Digital camera
- Photography budget.

Compiled with Helen Elias.

APPENDIX C

Framework agreements

Framework agreements have their origin in the 'term commissions' developed by the Ministry of Defence in the mid-1980s. Many still use these labels interchangeably, and some struggle to explain the difference between the two. Definitions are tricky because frameworks and term commissions can vary considerably from one client to another. The classic difference is that term commissions are deals reached with just one consultant or architect; framework agreements, which started to emerge in the mid-1990s, are signed with a whole range of different practices, or even teams of consultants.

Essentially, though, a framework agreement represents a formal, long-term relationship between a client and a small number of practices who can look forward to repeat work over the lifetime of the contract.

There is no standard model for a framework agreement. In one model, the client signs up a wide range of independent consultants – from architects and engineers to contractors and carpet suppliers – and compiles a team according to the needs of a particular project. In another model, the opposite is the case. The client appoints just lead consultants on the basis that they already have a viable team of subcontractors and other professional expertise in place. In this case, the client signs up a number of predetermined teams and hands out work according to that team's area of expertise.

There is a third variation. Some clients expect framework teams to come complete with their own project manager. Others prefer to appoint a project manager of their own.

Frameworks are typically found in the public sector (like the NHS), or among bodies that are publicly regulated (like BAA). But these contracts do occur in the private sector, too, and they run in much the same way. The Royal Bank of Scotland and IT firms Cisco and PeopleSoft, for example, operate framework agreements.

The advantages of frameworks are clear. For the architect, signing an agreement means they could be securing a close relationship with a client for a period of around 5–7 years. Being one of just a few architects signed up by, say, the Foreign and Commonwealth Office is a proud boast and the prospect of repeat work from such a client is an alluring one.

But most of the advantages lie with the client. Having signed a framework agreement, the client is under no obligation to guarantee work. They may even, for specialist or very large jobs, appoint an architect who is outside the agreement. Clients also get a good price – architects often offer very competitive rates in order to get on to the framework. As well as all that, framework agreements generally contain a tough list of key performance indicators, which if they aren't met, allow the client to terminate the agreement at any time. Importantly, framework agreements free clients from embarking on expensive selection processes every time a project comes up. But this also benefits the architects – they don't have to market themselves each time a job materializes. They've already done that.

Aedas management structure

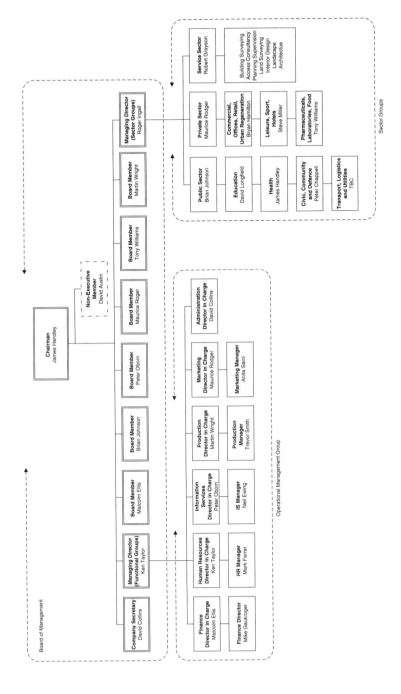

Figure A.1 Aedas Board of Management organization chart.

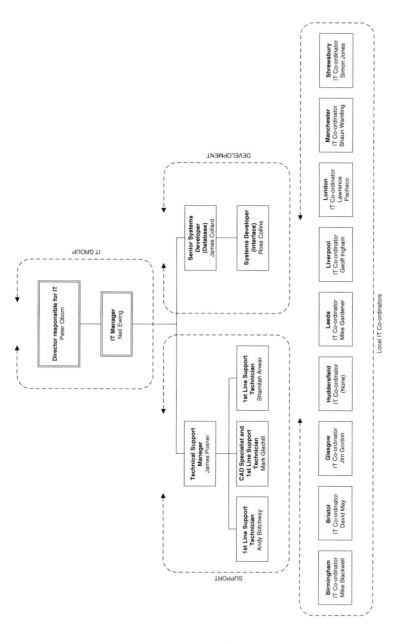

Figure A.2 Aedas Information Services organization chart.

APPENDIX E

Employment contracts

All employers must provide staff with a copy of their employment terms within 2 months of their starting a job. A comprehensive contract is useful because it allows an employer to communicate to a new employee exactly (a) the terms under which they have been employed; and (b) what their duties and responsibilities are. The contract also gives the employer the chance to mention miscellaneous matters such as dress-code and codes regarding the use of, for example, the internet. A full description of what is required under the law – the Employment Rights Act 1996 – can be found at www.hmso.gov.uk/acts/acts1996/1996018.htm.

A contract should include the following:

- Name and address of the employer and employee, and the address of the place of work (if different from the head office location).
- The date on which employment commences (and completes, if a job is only temporary).
- Gross salary and the date on which an employee is to be paid, with details of profit-share schemes and pension arrangements.

Payment intervals must also be included (e.g. whether payments are weekly or monthly).

- Holidays and a statement covering sick leave, compassionate leave, etc. Practices may also wish to have a policy covering an employee's ability to add unused holidays to a new year's allowance.
- Notice period.
- Job title and job description (and, if relevant, details of an appraisal scheme).
- Working hours and details of flexitime/overtime arrangements.
- Details of a probationary period.
- Description of allowable expenses.
- Restrictions. For example, a practice may wish to prevent staff from undertaking their own private commissions (or, a practice may consent to such commissions, so long as they are undertaken outside office hours and without using office resources).
- Disciplinary procedure.
- Intellectual property rights. Practices may wish to set out clearly that any work undertaken by an employee is done on behalf of the practice, therefore intellectual property rights belong to the practice.
- Statement covering student work experience – including study leave, mentoring and time off for exams.

Practice administration

Administration – covering everything from invoicing, timesheets, payroll, archiving and contact management – is rarely done well in architectural offices. Locating even very basic information in large, well-resourced practices can often be time-consuming and frustrating. With care, and the help of some useful software packages, sound administration can help practices save both money and time.

The signature of a good administration system is being able to conduct an 'audit trail', which means being able to find out who did what and when they did it. It is not uncommon for an architect to spend at least half an hour every day trying to locate files, phone numbers or even basic project data. Even during a live project, architects often find it difficult to recall key data – and when a project is more than a couple of years old, information can become so embedded in a bureaucratic labyrinth that locating it is a matter of luck.

A database of key project information is essential. Once in place, the database can help a practice quickly assess itself against a range of key performance indicators: cost-efficient projects, profitable sectors, productive teams, reliable suppliers and so on. Also, databases allow a practice to rapidly put together a bid for work; by retrieving data from past projects, a convincing, detailed and customized document can be delivered within a couple of days (or less). Imagine a potential client requesting, out of the blue, examples of your work on, say, social housing – there is no reason why you shouldn't be able to email a complete set of jpegs/PDFs and brief project descriptions within half an hour. Sending a mixture of file formats (including some the client cannot translate) a week later is just not good enough.

Software which does absolutely everything a practice needs is not (yet) available, but good programs do exist which can add real value to the running of a practice (some of which are web-based). Equally, there are some excellent programmers, with an architectural background, who can write bespoke packages. The result is that mistakes are minimized or, at least, a mistake that has been made can easily be tracked down and dealt with.

Importantly, different administration systems should be integrated as far as possible. Larger practices have invested huge sums in systems which bring together drawings, document templates, supplier information, project management stages and even payroll information. The result is that practices develop an efficient and predictable way of working, that they can easily prove their value to a client, that invoices are chased when appropriate and that official documentation is written to pre-determined standards.

Ultimately, sound administration can make the difference between winning or losing a job. And with larger jobs, clients want to know that you can handle the paperwork, as well as the design challenges.

Business management and accounting software

MYOB
0845 130 3975
customerservice@myob.co.uk
www.myob.com

Sage
0800 44 77 77
newbusinessadvice@sage.com
www.sage.co.uk

Practice administration

Autotrac Architect
0845 456 0546
alan.sheridan@autotrac-architect.co.uk
www.autotrac-architect.co.uk

Cosential (US web-based system now becoming available in the UK)
+1 203.762.9517
sales@Cosential.com
www.cosential.com

Time monitoring/billing/costing

JMS 2000 (Job Management System)
01453 768180
sales@job-management-systems.com
www.job-management-systems.com

TIMEminder
01273 748200
www.ph-media.com

Data management and archiving

Open Asset
01223 464697
www.axomic.com

Planchest
enquiries@planchest.net
www.planchest.net

Portfolio
01604 636300
www.extensis.com

Knowledge/Project management

Archetype
info@archsoft.co.uk
www.archsoft.co.uk/
www.oasys-software.com

prAxis
01698 404540
mike.dunning@isisys.com
www.isisys.com

Workspace
0115 9501020
www.unionsquaresoftware.com

Business models

There are four principal types of corporate set up – the public limited company (PLC), the private limited company (e.g. Joe Bloggs Ltd), the limited liability partnership (LLP) and the standard partnership where partners are effectively self-employed. There are literally only one or two PLCs in the architectural profession (Aukett is the best known) and that corporate format does not really concern us here.

There are considerable advantages to the other three business models – all are different, and each comes with pros and cons. Each model could easily be the subject of an entire book and space does not allow a full examination of the subject in this one. Any architect should consult with both an accountant and a lawyer in order to make a decision about whether to incorporate as a limited company or register as an LLP.

The default business model is the basic partnership, and most practices begin in this way. In brief, there are two advantages and two disadvantages to partnerships. On the plus side, they are easy to set up and they require no public declaration of earnings (your earnings are between you and the tax inspector).

On the minus side, the partnership is not recognized as a legal entity in itself, so the partners face unlimited liability in the event of a claim being made against the practice. Also, standard partnerships attract no special tax breaks or concessions.

At the other end of the spectrum is the limited company. As mentioned in Chapter 1, accountants will generally advise you to explore this route, if only for the tax advantages (which are gradually being tightened up). Apart from that, companies *are* legal entities, so any claim made against the practice is made against the company and not individuals within it. Limited companies therefore afford greater protection to their founders. On the other hand, suppliers are fully aware of the protective veil provided by company status and they may want paying in advance for a period of time before a sufficient level of trust is established. Another disadvantage is that administration is more time-consuming, and company accounts have to be filed (and made public) annually. This is, however, an attractive option for many practices: John McAslan & Partners, Alsop Architects, Eva Jiricna and MacCormack Jamieson Pritchard are all limited companies.

The last, and newest, option is the LLP. Limited liability partnerships were made possible by the LLP Act in 2000 and have become widely adopted in other professions, such as law and accountancy. Leading law firms including Allen & Overy and Clifford Chance have become LLPs.

Essentially, an LLP falls somewhere between a partnership and a limited company. The LLP is a legal entity and, as its name suggests, limits the liability of its partners (referred to in the legislation as 'members'). An LLP is still managed as a partnership and is taxed as one. It is, however, transparent for tax and earnings purposes – audited accounts have to be filed which disclose the earnings of the highest paid members, as well as annuities to retired members. Some practices may feel awkward about having to engage in such financial openness.

An article by solicitor Caroline Williams (then of law firm Browne Jacobson) which appeared in the *RIBA Journal* in

October 2002 warns, however, that the limited liability of LLPs is not watertight. If, for example, a member gives a client any personal guarantees or accepts specific personal responsibilities beyond those covered by the LLP, then that member could well be personally liable for any claim. Also, Williams points out that practices need to be aware of the admininstrative burden of becoming an LLP.

'There is a considerable amount of work involved in transfering employees, assets and contracts to the new entity. One critical area will be the renewal of contracts with clients, clarifying that members did not have a personal duty of care to the client, to limit the risk of claim against an individual member of the LLP,' said Williams. 'A major public relations exercise might need to be carried out to reassure all parties with whom the firm has a relationship that it is "business as usual" and the switch has no adverse consequences for them.'

Nonetheless, a small number of architectural practices have made the move to LLP status, including: Sidell Gibson, MAE, Knox Bhaven Architects and McNeil Beechey O'Neill Architects. If a practice makes the conversion to LLP status without their landlord or bank requiring personal guarantees of liability, then the move is probably a wise one and the security is worth the administrative effort.

Readers must be aware that this article is not intended to represent legal or financial advice. Practices wishing to explore these issues further are advised to speak to the RIBA and their professional advisers. Law firm Browne Jacobson, which became an LLP on 1 May 2004, continues to provide advice on this subject – call Iain Blatherwick on 0115 976 6183.

Details about LLPs can also be found at www.legalpulse.com and www.legal-term.com. Standard partnership agreements can also be downloaded, for a fee of approximately £30.

Contacts

Accountants

Stanes Rand
10 Jesus Lane,
Cambridge, Cambridgeshire, CB5 8BA
01223 461 044
E-mail: stanesrand@aol.com
www.stanesrand.co.uk

Sobell Rhodes
Chartered Accountants
215 Marsh Road, Pinner, Middlesex HA5 5NE
020 8866 2151
www.sobellrhodes.co.uk

Gorman Seaton
74 Chancery Lane, London WC1 1AA
0207 8313125
Email: gorman-seaton@talk21.com

Lawyers

39 Essex Street (planning specialists)
London WC2R 3AT

020 7832 1111
clerks@39essex.com
www.39essex.com

Eversheds (worldwide reputation for HR and employment)
Senator House
85 Queen Victoria Street
London EC4V 4JL
020 7919 4500
www.eversheds.com

Denton Wilde Sapte
5 Chancery Lane,
Clifford's Inn,
London EC4A 1BU
020 7242 1212
email: info@dentonwildesapte.com
www.dentonwildesapte.com

Mayer Brown Rowe
11 Pilgrim Street
London EC4V 6RW
020 7248 4282
www.mayerbrownrowe.com

Business advice, HR, practice management

Federation of Small Businesses
Sir Frank Whittle Way
Blackpool Business Park
Blackpool, Lancashire FY4 2FE
01253 336000
www.fsb.org.uk

Chartered Institute of Personnel and Development
CIPD House
Camp Road
London SW19 4UX

020 8971 9000
www.cipd.co.uk

Investors in People
7–10 Chandos Street
London, W1G 9DQ
020 7467 1900.
www.iipuk.co.uk

The Creative Support Agency (office management services)
49–51 Central Street
London, EC1V 8AB
07958 555571
www.creativesupportagency.co.uk

Networking

www.vectorworks.co.uk/index2.html
www.spa.uk.net/network.htm
www.acanthus.co.uk
www.bentleyuser.org
www.riba.org
www.architectyourhome.com

IT consultants/Trainers

Jonathan Reeves Architecture
0117 9711359
0771 3633205
email: jonathan.reeves@blueyonder.co.uk
www.jrarchitecture.pwp.blueyonder.co.uk

Croser Consulting
Contact: Joe Croser
07973 263360 e joe@croser.net
www.croser.net

i2i Information and Technology Consultancy
Contact: Stephen Pacey
01962 810430
Email: stephen.pacey@i2it.biz
www.i2it.biz

Lomas Davies
07950200461
Email: mail@lomasdavies.net
www.lomasdavies.net

CICA
Construction Industry Computing Association
1 Trust Court, Histon, Cambridge CB4 9PW
01223 236 336
E-mail: postmaster@cica.org.uk
www.cica.org.uk

Marketing, PR, Press relations

Tamesis
73 Wimpole street
London W1G 8AZ
020 7908 3200
www.tamesis-pr.com

Northern Assurance Building
Princess Street
Manchester M2 4DN
0161 834 3834

Laura Iloniemi Architectural Press and PR
Studio102
Westbourne Studios
242 Acklam Road
London W10 5JJ
020 7575 3175
e-mail: laura@iloniemi.co.uk

Atelier Communications
Contact: Helen Elias
01225 869 470
helen@ateliercommunications.co.uk

Stratton & Reekie
46 Broadwick Street
London W1F 7AF
020 7287 8456
email: areekie@strattonandreekie.com

Caro Communications
19/20 Great Sutton Street
London EC1V 0DR
020 7336 8488
email: pr@carocommunications.com
www.carocommunications.com

Camargue
www.camarguepr.com
7 Bayley Street
London WC1B 3HB
020 7636 7366
and
Wellington Road
Cheltenham GL52 2AG
01242 577 277

Wordsearch (architectural marketing and communications consultancy)
5 Old Street
London EC1V 9HL
020 7549 5400
www.wordsearch.co.uk

Index